MW00388220

From Beer to Eternity

Louisville, Kentucky, circa 1895
(Photo courtesy University of
Louisville Photographic Archives,
Caufield & Shook Collection)

FROM BEER TO ETERNITY

Everything You Always Wanted to Know about Beer

Will Anderson

The Stephen Greene Press

LEXINGTON, MASSACHUSETTS

First published in 1987 by The Stephen Greene Press, Inc.
Published simultaneously in Canada by Penguin Books Canada Limited
Distributed by Viking Penguin Inc., 40 West 23rd Street, New York, NY 10010.

Line drawings on pages 7, 13, 15, 50, 62, 63, 66, 67, 126, 136, 144, 145, 146, 147 by Darlene Michaud.
Line drawings on pages 57, 107, 136 by Judith Love.
All artwork not otherwise credited is from the author's collection.

Library of Congress Cataloging-in-Publication Data
Anderson, Will
    From beer to eternity.

    1. Beer.   I. Title.
TP577.A534   1987   641.2′3   86-32016
ISBN 0-8289-0555-X

Designed by Joyce C. Weston
Printed in the United States of America
by Alpine Press
Set in Century Expanded and Benguait Condensed
Produced by Unicorn Production Services, Inc.

From Beer to Eternity is lovingly dedicated
to my sons, Carl and Curt.

It is said that a man unto whom
a son is born is a blessed man.
I am twice blessed.

Acknowledgments

In researching and writing *From Beer to Eternity*, I was fortunate enough to have been helped by a lot of wonderful people. I'd like to especially thank: Edward I. Barz, Simmons Market Research Bureau, Inc., New York City; Joseph Blackstock, Foster and Kleiser, Los Angeles; Mac Brighton, *Modern Brewery Age*, Stamford, Connecticut; Don Bull, Stamford, Connecticut; Mary Lou Chianese, Sundor Group, Inc., Darien, Connecticut; Terry Christopherson, G. Heileman Brewing Co., LaCrosse, Wisconsin; Pat Connelly, Doubleday Book Clubs, New York City; Adolph Coors Co., Golden, Colorado; John Corrado, Purdys, New York; Erin Dunn, John F. Kennedy Center for the Performing Arts, Washington, D.C.; Leonard Faupel, Short Hills, New Jersey; Augie Helms, Union, New Jersey; Ed Hogan, Jones Brewing Co., Smithton, Pennsylvania; R.A. Horvath, Miller Brewing Co., Milwaukee; Vic, Tom, and Bob Hug, Lorain, Ohio; Phil Katz, The Beer Institute, Washington, D.C.; Barbara Lessman, Cleveland Indians, Cleveland; Laura Longley, John F. Kennedy Center for the Performing Arts, Washington, D.C.; Renae Marley, New York City; Fritz Maytag, Anchor Brewing Co., San Francisco; Jack McDougall, Bar Tourists of America, Cranford, New Jersey; Mary and John Milkovisch, Houston; Ed Nichols, Brooklyn; Gary Nowlin, Allentown, Pennsylvania; "Uncle" Ernie Oest, Port Jefferson Station, New York; Bill Owens, Buffalo Bill's Brewery and Brewpub, Hayward, California; Charlie Papazian, American Homebrewers Assn., Boulder, Colorado; Mike Rissetto, Floral Park, New York; Francie Patton, Hudepohl-Schoenling Brewing Co., Cincinnati; Manny Toreces, Toreces' Pantry, New York City; Wm. Vollmar, Anheuser-Busch, Inc., St. Louis; Jim Welytok, Milwaukee; Kurt and Rob Widmer, Widmer Brewing Co., Portland, Oregon; Keith Wiarda, New York Yankees, Bronx, New York; Karen Wiecha, The Stroh Brewery Co., Detroit; David "Santa" Williams, San Diego; and, finally, Dick Yuengling, D. G. Yuengling & Son, Pottsville, Pennsylvania.

From me to you all: the very best of a frosty, foamy one!

Contents

Introduction

As far back as I can recall, I've been a collector of something or other. Some of my earliest childhood memories revolve around collecting liberty head coins. Going through my father's change when he came home from work in the evening, and my grandmother's getting her local theaters and restaurants to pull them out for me are experiences I can still readily—and pleasurably—call to mind.

Stickball, Stanley Jones, and Gus Zernial

From coins I graduated to baseball cards. How could I do otherwise: I lived in Yonkers, New York, in a neighborhood that seemed to live, breathe, eat, and sleep baseball (translate stickball: most of the time we didn't have enough room or there were too many windows for hardball). When I wasn't powering doubles down the left field line, I was scrounging up money to buy— and buy and buy—endless packs of baseball cards. When a new shipment came into Rich's Corner Candy Store, it was almost as exciting as a day off from P.S. 14. And I didn't even like the bubble gum!

In 1951, my mother and father—in their infinite wisdom—decided that Yonkers was no longer a fit place to raise my kid sister, Carol, and myself. We were to move to lily green Ardsley, farther up the line in Westchester County. The last day before the move was a terrifying one for me. What ten-year-old wants to leave behind his

buddies . . . not to mention his stickball and corner candy store connections? But Stanley Jones eased the pain. Stanley, a year older and generally a stickball rival, presented me with a gift. It was a small box, a box he'd wrapped himself. In it was a single baseball card. A Gus Zernial card. Old "Ozark Ike," a powerhitting but leadfooted (and pretty much leadgloved, too) outfielder for the White Sox and Athletics (the *Philadelphia* Athletics!), was the only card I was missing to complete my entire 1951 set. No one around had even *seen* a Gus Zernial. But now I *had* one. Needless to say, I still do. Thanks, Stanley Jones.

It's Only Rock 'n Roll

It took a long while for me to get used to Ardsley. No one played stickball. And if you collected baseball cards, you collected them alone.

But then it happened. In early 1955, some cool cat in the back of the school bus started talking about this crazy new music. Said it was called rock 'n roll. Said to tune into WINS and listen to the sounds being put down by a DJ named Alan Freed. So I did. It took about five songs and I was a rock 'n roller. Hello Fats Domino, Bo Diddley, Shirley & Lee, Bill Haley & the Comets, Johnny Ace, the Moonglows, Spaniels, Cardinals, Fitones, Solitaires. Goodbye Eddie Fisher, Patti Page, Joni James, Perry Como, Rosemary Clooney. Just about every

Frank Thomas

Willie Mays

Dick Groat

A DAY AT THE POLO GROUNDS. The author with idols Frank Thomas (my older son is named Carl *Thomas* Anderson), Willie Mays, and Dick Groat on a summer's day in 1955. My cousin Eddie McCarrick—obviously my favorite cousin—was a scout for the Pirates: he'd invited me to come on down to the ballpark early and meet some of the players.

It's a day one doesn't forget. Ever.

FIFTIES' FAVORITES. Has there been a teenager anytime/any-place who hasn't had his or her favorite recording artists? Fifties' favorites in my neck of the New York suburbs (meaning *my* favorites!) included "The Fabulous Fat Man from New Orleans," Fats Domino, and a now largely forgotten (but nevertheless very fine) vocal group from the streets of Brooklyn, the Four Fellows.

Saturday, my girlfriend Kendree and I would somehow get to the area's shopping hub, White Plains . . . and its record stores, Hunt's and Burt & Walker. In those days, most record stores had listening booths: you could grab a stack of 45's, go in the booth (nice and cozy for two!), and pretty much play records as long as you wanted . . . as long as you eventually bought at least a couple of them. That was no problem. I always bought at least two or three; often six or eight or ten. I was a rock 'n roll record collector!

Rock 'n roll and record collecting has never left my blood. I still love to thumb through old 45's at tag, garage, and (as they're called in Brooklyn) stoop sales. Through the years I've accumulated a good five or six thousand of them. And I even programmed and hosted a weekly three-hour 1950s rock 'n roll/rhythm and blues radio show over (irony of ironies!) WINE-FM, Brookfield-Danbury, Connecticut, for four years—from 1971 through 1975. Dedications, specials, guest vocal groups, great music . . . and great fun!

But It's Beer, Beer, Beer That Really Makes Me Want to Cheer

In the fall of 1961, early in my senior year at Cornell University, a fraternity brother of mine, greatly annoyed because his date had stood him up on a big party weekend, proceeded to knock off close to a case of cans of Ballantine Beer. As he drank them, he stacked them in a pyramid. Later in the week one of my roommates, Bob Myers, and I got to wondering how many brands of canned beer there were. We decided to drive around Ithaca to see how many we could get, picked up something like twenty-six . . . and became beer can collectors.

Actually we became fanatical beer can collectors! We thought we were the only "nuts" in the world who cared more about the can than what was in it . . . so naturally we had to do the work of many. We started cutting Friday classes to take off on weekend beer can treks. Boston, Montreal, Washington, Detroit, Chicago, Milwaukee . . . we "covered" them all, plus a lot of places in between. Did our grades suffer? They sure did. Did we much care? Nope; adding to our collection was much more important.

Cans eventually led to my getting interested in pre-Prohibition (i.e., pre-1920) embossed beer bottles. I became fascinated with the fact that, back in the beginning years of this very century, just about every American city and town of any consequence had its own brewery, its own beer. And many had their own embossed (i.e., raised lettering) bottles, too. Plus, packaging showmen that they've tended to be, a fair number of brewers featured elaborate designs in addition to bold lettering.

I poked around bottle shows and bought and traded with other bottle buffs across the country. But mostly my ex-wife, Sonja, and I would go bottle digging. Poking around old dump sites was many a weekend's great adventure; you never knew what your next shovelful would unearth. Sometimes a bottle, sometimes a snake, sometimes nothing. Poison ivy was the one constant. From there it was on to beer trays. Handed out by the thousands by breweries to bars and restaurants from the 1890s until just recently, these gems of

FROM CANS TO BOTTLES TO...

From beer cans...

to beer bottles...   to beer trays...

to beer posters...

to what you're holding in your hand right now... my favorite (and hopefully yours, too) collection of beer facts, folklore, and fun.

advertising art were meant to be used to serve foaming glasses of beer (preferably the donor brewery's beer!). Fortunately, many of them escaped that sure road to rust and ruination. I searched for them just about everywhere: at flea markets and garage sales, in antique shops, even in deserted breweries. My favorites were those that showed a view of the brewery itself (generally always with flags flying and smokestacks belching... to show both patriotism and industriousness) or the "girlie" art so popular in the 1930s and 1940s. Another great love was—and is—the beautifully lithographed calendars put out by brewers both large and small prior to Prohibition. Extremely ornate and colorful, these beauties were designed to adorn taproom walls. But I soon concluded that they didn't look bad adorning my breweriana room walls either. In fact, they looked great!

Probably my strongest beer/breweriana enthusiasm, however, has been the desire to collect as much information as possible about the wonderful folklore and history of American beer, and beer's quite significant contribution to our culture and fabric. The result: a series of books, starting away back in 1968, on beer and breweries and breweriana that I have loved writing and I hope folks have enjoyed reading. *From Beer to Eternity* is the culmination of them all. The "coup de brew," if you will.

I very much hope you enjoy it!

"I have taken more out of alcohol than alcohol has taken out of me."
— *Winston Churchill*

From Beer to Eternity

"'Did you ever taste beer?' 'I had a sip
of it once,' said the small servant.
'Here's a state of things!' cried Mr.
Swiveller . . . 'She *never* tasted it—it
can't be tasted in a sip!'"
                              — Charles Dickens
                              Nicholas Nickleby

What Is This Thing Called Beer?

Beer, as a word, comes from the Latin *bibere*, to drink. But what is it exactly that you're drinking when you're drinking beer? To give you a heightened appreciation of your favorite beverage, let's take a quickie course on what goes into beer and how it all comes together during the brewing process.

Here, from a United States Brewers Association booklet entitled *The Story of Beer*, is the lowdown on how it all happens.

The story begins with grain — choice barley from farms in North Dakota, South Dakota, Minnesota, California, and other midwestern and West Coast states. This grain is so good that farmers receive a premium price for it.

Before it reaches the brewery, the barley goes to the malt industry to be turned into malt ("Malt" is a word that comes from the old Anglo-Saxon "mealt," meaning "meal.").

When you plant a seed in the springtime, the dampness in the earth and the warmth of the sun cause it to come to life and sprout. The scientific word for this mysterious happening in vegetable life is "germination."

Barley, given just the right amounts of moisture and warmth to make it germinate, becomes malt. The inner goodness of the kernel comes to full peak, ready to sprout and grow.

The malting or germination of barley brings about, inside the grain, a rapid increase of juices called "enzymes." Nature places them in fruits and vegetables to help the plants absorb food. Enzymes speed the change of a substance from one form to another. A common enzyme in the stomach, pepsin, aids your digestion by helping change the food you eat into chemicals your body needs.

Malt at the Brewery

The duty of malt and its enzymes at the brewery is to transform grain starches into soft starch-sugar (*maltose*). Thus the second chapter in the story of beer begins at the malt and cereal storage bins of the brewery, where amounts of these grains are measured out as carefully as your mother measures flour and sugar in making a cake.

Of ourse, instead of working with cupfuls, the brewmaster's recipe calls for hundreds of pounds at a time. The malt is mixed with

HERE'S TO BEER. Workers at the Jacob Ruppert Brewery in New York City toasting the return of legal beer, March 1933. (Photo courtesy *New York News*)

pure, heated water in a big *mash* tub and stirred until the kernels, softened by the movement of the warm water, come apart.

Meanwhile, other grains (corn or rice) are boiled in big cookers and added to the malt mash. In the mash tub the enzymes, "digesting" the grain starches, change the starch into maltose sugar.

Both the starch and its new form, maltose, contain the same elements of carbon, hydrogen, and oxygen. That is, both are *carbohydrates*. Due to the work of the enzymes, however, the molecules have been shifted and regrouped to make the sugar slightly different from the starch in taste, texture, and other qualities.

A Touch of Flavor

The mash mixture next flows into the *lauter tub*, which looks like a huge cylinder and which contains strainers and filters. These remove the empty barley hulls, bits of corn kernels, and similar grain particles no longer needed. (These grains, rich in protein, are sold by brewers as livestock feed.)

With these grains removed, what is left is a clear liquid called *wort* (pronounced "wurt"). This mixture of maltose and water has a sweet taste with the savor of cereal. For added flavor it is now run into giant copper kettles to be brewed with hops.

Continued on next page

1

ONLY FEMALE HOPS NEED APPLY. Turn-of-the-century trade card from Dole Brothers, dealers in malt and hops.

Hops, used to give beer its distinctive taste, come, not surprisingly, from the hop plant. What may come as a surprise is the knowledge that the plant is *dioecious*, the male and female flowers are borne on separate plants. Only the female flowers are used in the flavoring of beer, and great care is taken to ensure that they do not come in contact with pollen from the male plant. If this happens and the seeds become fertilized, they develop a bitter and unpleasant taste.

Hops are the dried, cone-like fruit of vines grown mostly on farms in West Coast states.... The brewmaster takes care that only the best-quality hops, in exact amounts, are used. He keeps close track of the temperature and length of brewing time since these factors affect the flavor and color of the beer.

After the hops are strained off, the wort now has its unique flavor and amber color. Still boiling hot, the liquid is pumped to cooling tanks on the top floor of the brewery, where its temperature drops from 212° to 180°. For further cooling—with the help of gravity—the wort is allowed to pour downward over refrigerated coils so that its temperature is around 50° when it next enters the *starter* tank.

At this stage another curious change begins to take place, because carefully-measured amounts of yeast are added to the liquid. Here a new chapter in the story of beer begins.

Thousands of years ago, man discovered that the presence of tiny gas bubbles in a drink—*effervescence*—helped it to quench thirst.

Eventually, somebody learned that yeast can give liquid a natural carbonation; thus, in making beer, creating tiny bubbles and foam.

"The Controlled Miracle"

Yeast looks like a soft, creamy mass, something like cream cheese. Actually this is a mass of millions of cells of plant-like life containing another enzyme. Aided by its enzyme, yeast "eats" maltose and grows by budding.

In digesting the starch-sugar, yeast breaks down the sugar and creates two new substances, carbon dioxide which provides the carbonation and alcohol.

This step in making beer is the same one that takes place when yeast acts on the starch-sugar of wheat to *leaven* (meaning "to make light") a loaf of bread or tin of dinner rolls. The carbon dioxide gas causes the dough to "rise." The alcohol evaporates during baking.

The yeast action is called *fermentation*. In the fermentation tanks at the brewery, yeast is allowed to work on the starch-sugar for carefully controlled lengths of time and under closely guarded temperatures.

Beer flavor, the amount of alcohol and other qualities of the beverage depend a great deal on the exact, scientific handling of the yeast. Expertly trained people and sensitive, automatic equipment achieve this "controlled miracle," as the brewing industry's use of yeast has been termed.

Every brewery has its own prized strain of yeast. Many varieties were brought to America from Europe years ago and have been passed down from one generation to another. Like the specially grown malt barley and the carefully selected hops, the yeast which a brewer uses does its part in influencing the character of the beer being made.

For this reason breweries operate costly laboratories where research men are always studying the yeast, as well as testing the grains, mashes, and wort at various stages of brewing.

Near the Journey's End

After the yeast has done its proper amount of work, it is removed and the beer pumped into *aging tanks*. These are large, stainless-steel storage tanks where the beer is kept at a cool temperature for many weeks. "Lager" is a term often used for this aging process, during which particles of remaining yeast settle to the bottom and the beer slowly grows crystal clear.

As the beer nears its time to be marketed, it is given a final carbonation treatment. This is done with some of the same carbon dioxide that was given off during fermentation, was collected and saved for this purpose. Another carbonation method is to mix a small amount of fermenting beer in the aging tank. Either way, the brewery brings the carbonation to the exact point of natural effervescence that it desires.

With a final filtering, the beer is now ready for "packaging" in barrel, bottle, or can.

More important the beer is now ready to be enjoyed by its public. Prosit!

OUR BABY

YES, SIR, THAT'S MY BABY. Although brewing has become much, much more scientific and controlled over the past century, today's brewmaster more than likely still feels about his beer the way our friend here did about 1890 ... it's his "baby."

The Brewery That Died for Its Country

The brewery that died for its country. That dubious honor goes to the former Lion Brewery of New York City. Located on the upper reaches of now super chic Columbus Avenue, Lion once roared with the best of them. In the 1870s, then known as Bernheimer & Schmid's Lion Brewery, it consistently ranked among the nation's largest brewers.

But times change. Lions — and breweries — sometimes wind down. After Prohibition the Lion Brewery was just a shadow of its former self. It limped along until 1942, then closed down. Two years later the brewery made the ultimate sacrifice: over three thousand tons of structural steel were recovered from the brewery, dismantled by the War Production Board for war scrap.

The Lion Brewery of New York City as it appeared in 1909, several years before our first less-than-friendly encounter with Germany.

Where Have All the Brewers Gone?

A graph of the number of brewers in operation in America over the last one hundred years looks not unlike the Cyclone ride at Coney Island: a few ups, but mostly straight down.

In 1880 we had 2,272 breweries doing their thing with barley and hops and water. Almost every town of any consequence had at least one brewery of its own; larger cities generally had many. Beer was basically a *local* product.

Slightly over a century later, we have less than one hundred breweries in operation. Very few towns of consequence or not have a brewery of their own. Even some of our very largest cities do not. Beer is basically a *national* product.

From 2,272 breweries to 95 breweries: the story of the U.S. brewing industry over the past one hundred plus years. And even the 95 is misleading. Many of these are branch breweries, part of a chain. There were, in reality, only 63 brewing companies in operation in 1985.

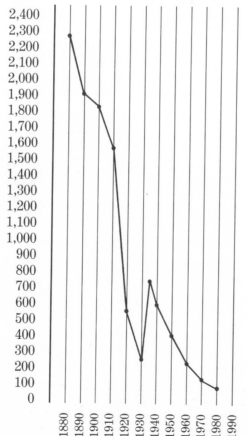

Number of U.S. Brewers in Operation
1880–1985

Where have all the brewers gone? Out of business. The reasons why are many.

Prohibition, of course, took a tremendous toll. Legislate an entire industry out of commission for fourteen years and you're going to flatten a lot of sales curves. But the brewing industry was changing well before America's dry spell arrived on the scene in 1920.

• Pasteur's discovery, in 1876, that the flash heating of beer killed bacteria that so often caused spoilage was a boon to the bottling of beer.
• The development of an efficient transcontinental railway system (followed later by a nationwide highway system) allowed that bottled beer to be transported hither and yon across the far reaches of the nation with not a heck of a lot more difficulty than transporting it hither and yon across the less than far reaches of Ohio or Missouri or Wisconsin.
• Federal regulations with respect to the bottling of beer were made much less inane in the early 1890s. These changes were of a much greater help to the larger "shipping" brewer than to his smaller mostly-draft-sold-locally counterpart.

By Prohibition, then, America's brewing ranks had already been thinned considerably. The year 1918 would see the last time we ever had over one thousand active breweries.

During Prohibition most brewers gave it the old college try by doing their best to keep things going via near beer, soft drinks, ice cream, and/or fruit drinks. Schlitz manufactured candy and chocolates; Blatz tried its hand at industrial alcohol; Coors did well with malted milk; Anheuser-Busch experimented with a whole host of products, the most successful of which was yeast; Yuengling brewed up an elixir named Juvetonic.

But plant closings mostly filled the brewery trade papers during the 1920s. Breweries, being built like brick malthouses, made for good storage facilities. Many an

4

XXX Brewing Company became an XXX Moving and Storage Company. Some breweries were put to less obvious use: the Flint Brewing Co. in Flint, Michigan, became a Methodist church.

Then came repeal!

After all the hullabaloo died down, somewhat over seven hundred brewers began to roll out the barrels again. Many of the seven hundred plus were undercapitalized and/or poorly managed, however. Physical plant and equipment were, in far too many cases, obsolete or close to it and, as before Prohibition, other factors tended to favor the bigs.

- The introduction of the beer can in 1935 triggered the start of the no deposit/no return packaging revolution. No longer did a brewery in St. Louis or Milwaukee have to be bothered with getting empties back from Walla Walla or Weehawken or anywhere in between. And the lighter, more compact can was much easier and more economical than bottles (then all long-neck) to ship in the first place.
- National radio—and later national television—led to national advertising: big-time ad budgets that helped to make big-time brewers even bigger.
- There have been and continue to be economies of scale: the bigger the firm = the bigger the purchase = the bigger the discount.

Plug into all of the above, and you don't need an electronic scoreboard to know the game's outcome. The United States brewing industry is presently dominated by a handful of giants.

But even roller coasters have a bottom . . . sometimes a rise. And thanks to the dedication and success of the microbrewery movement, we're now experiencing an increase in the number of operating brewers for the first time in a good fifty years.

Frank Jones Brewery, Portsmouth, New Hampshire, 1859-1950. Frank Jones, the man, was successful in politics as well as brewing. He served as a U.S. congressman for two terms, from 1875 to 1879.

Iroquois/International Brewing Co., Buffalo, 1892-1971. Buffalo: from nineteen breweries in 1910 to zero breweries in 1986.

M. K. Goetz Brewing Company, Kansas City, Missouri, 1936-1956. There is presently no beer "Made in Kansas City."

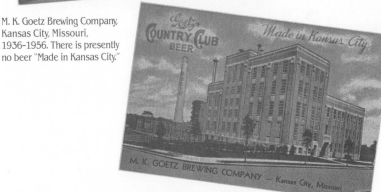

Hastings Brewing Co., Hastings, Nebraska, 1908-1917. When smoke—and plenty of it—was considered a sign of progress rather than a sign of pollution.

Why a Six-pack?

The Improved Tyte-Pack

"The Improved Tyte-Pack," manufactured by the Moulded Pulp Corp. of Chicago in the 1930s. Built to hold three bottles, its design featured a tight fit for protection and insulation to keep the bottles cool on their way home.

Why a six-pack? That's a question I get asked all the time. People stop me on the street corner and ask: "Why not an eight-pack or a four-pack or a fourteen-pack?"

It's a good question, one that warrants no easy — on the street corner — answer. The fact is that there's nothing truly magic about the number six. Ever since the beginnings of packaged beer, brewers have been striving to sell in multiple units. Selling a bunch of something beats selling one of it. But all kinds of "bunches" have been tried. Units of three, four, six, eight, and ten all had their advocates. The unit of six, however, seemed to work best.

Around 1938 or '39 we launched the beer can in a six-pack. The pack was built so you couldn't open the darn thing, it [the cardboard] was so heavy. Everything then was built to last forever!

I believe Ballantine was the first to use six-packs. I'm pretty confident of that. We had three-packs at one time, but when people bought beer — even without a pack — it tended to be in multiples of six. A full case was twenty-four. Six just seemed to be the way people would buy beer.
— *Leonard Faupel,*
Assistant Advertising Manager for P. Ballantine & Sons from 1938 to 1942 and from 1945 to 1955; Advertising Manager from 1956 to 1965

There are a couple of other reasons why six won out. After Prohibition, brewers found themselves increasingly marketing to women. Studies showed that the female of the household, generally responsible for the family's grocery shopping, was increasingly purchasing beer, just as she purchased butter and bread, as a grocery item for at-home consumption. The six-pack was the right weight; eight or ten were too heavy for the average woman. Also, Coca-Cola was being sold very successfully in units of six. Folks predisposed to buy soda

Those aren't shirts from the laundry that daddy's arriving home with in this 1934 photo. They're beer bottles wrapped the way they were in the days before convenience packaging.

"Do you know we sold ten bottles of White Label in a patented box called a Family-Pak for one dollar? The taverns didn't want to handle bottled beer. Everybody wanted draft beer. But we taught the guys [tavern owners] for Christmas to pile up five hundred of these at the end of the bar and ask people to buy them for their postman, their streetcleaner, etc. And I had grocers who put up signs: 'Make your Christmas gift Trommer's White Label Family-Pak.' "
— *Joseph Milgram, Advertising and Merchandising Manager for the John F. Trommer Brewing Co., Brooklyn, from 1933 to 1940*

A late 1933 ad from Container Corporation of America for its bottled beer six-pack "... built so you couldn't open the darn thing." Six was about the right weight for milady.

by the six-pack came to also be predisposed to buy beer by the six-pack.

Today there are still units of other than six. Champale, for one, comes in four-packs, and quite a number of brewers package their seven-ounce bottles in eight-packs. Twelve-packs and that favorite of generations of beer drinkers, the case of twenty-four, both have their supporters, too.

The six-pack, however, is the standard beer packaging unit. And now when someone comes up to you on the street corner and asks you why — Why a six-pack? — you can tell them why.

Better yet, bet them a six-pack you can tell them why. Then tell 'em!

"MORRIS TAKE HOME 6." By 1950, six-packs were starting to look sleek, even "sexy." This was a spring 1950 trade ad from Chicago's Morris Paper Mills for its "Morris Take Home 6."

Four Beers to One...

You can't name the rather famous former Yankee outfielder (183 home runs, 795 RBIs, and a .282 lifetime batting average for his eleven years in the bigs) who became the president of a brewery several years after his playing days were through.

Answer: "Old Reliable," Tommy Henrich, who became prexy of the Red Top Brewing Co., of Cincinnati in May 1954, 3½ years after his pinstripe days were over.

Albany Ale

There's a nice alliteration to Albany ale. And well there should be, for Albany and ale have long had a very meaningful relationship. Perhaps it's the lingering English-Irish tradition; perhaps it's the long winter's need for something hearty; perhaps it's the strong thirst of politics. Whatever it is, Albany has long enjoyed her ale, and people who like ale have long enjoyed Albany. Represented here are but a few of Albany's respected ale names from the past.

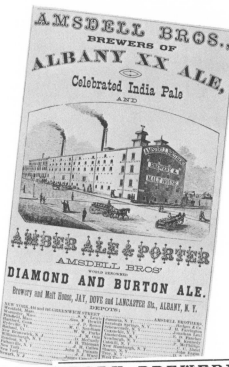

TAYLOR & SON, ALBANY IMPERIAL CREAM ALE,

BREWERY, 133 BROAD____ ____REET, ALBANY, N. Y.

DEPOTS—334 Greenwich St., New York; 117 Commer___ ____; 32 Fulton St., Brook___ ____rket St., Newark, N. J.

Agents in all t___ ___s of th___

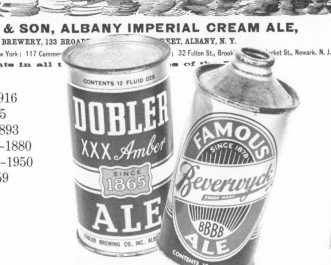

Amsdell: 1854–1916
Taylor: 1822–1905
Coleman: 1874–1893
A. S. Long: 1877–1880
Beverwyck: 1867–1950
Dobler: 1874–1959

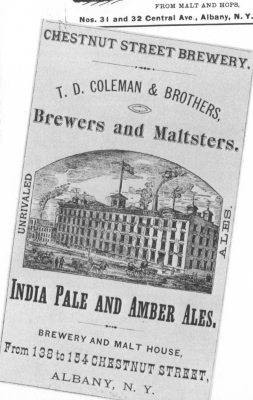

Even Ballantine — America's foremost ale name — got its start in Albany. Scottish emigrant Peter Ballantine began brewing ale in Albany in a modest way in 1833. Seven years later, craving a larger market, he moved to Newark. The rest, as they say, is history.

Carrying on Albany's ale-brewing tradition today is the Wm. S. Newman Brewing Co. Located in a former mattress factory on a dead-end street in the heart of industrial Albany, Newman has been producing fine ales — very fine, indeed — since 1981. If you're ever in the area, seek them out. It's worth the effort.

... And Anderson's Home Brewed Albany Ale

Some folks might say that a brewery that went out of business well over a hundred years ago doesn't warrant nearly a full half-page. But other folks know better!

ANDERSON & CO.'S HOME BREWED ALE,
FOR INVALIDS & FAMILY USE,
MADE OF MALT AND HOPS,
Cor. Green & Beaver Sts.,
ALBANY, N. Y.

Anderson & Co.'s announcement in the 1862 Albany City Directory: Ale so thick you probably needed a knife to cut it.

Anderson & Co.'s Home Brewed Ale: 1862–1872 What a Great Name!

9

Other Budweisers

Budweiser: nowadays it stands for "The King of Beers"; "This Bud's for You"; "When You've Said Budweiser, You've Said It All."

It stands for the largest selling beer in the world.

It stands for Anheuser-Busch.

But in days of not so long ago, it sometimes was also meant to stand for beer as brewed in Budweis, a city on the Vltava River in Bohemia (now Czechoslovakia). And it also was sometimes used to stand for — or stand in for — the most successful of all beer brewed as in Budweis, which, of course, brings us back to "The King of Beers" and so on: Budweiser as brewed by Anheuser-Busch.

Confusing, yes; but logical, too.

In the beginning was Carl Conrad and his luncheon in 1876, as told on page 153. Then came Adolphus Busch's gutsy — and very wise — decision to go national with Budweiser in bottles, as also told on page 153. Then came success.

Then came the inevitable . . . other Budweisers. By the 1890s there were at least four other major "Budweisers," plus a Budweis . . . and the longest lasting "other Budweiser" was yet to come.

When Brooklyn Had Its Own Budweiser

In 1884 a group of Brooklyn businessmen headed by a man named William Brown purchased the Bedford Brewery on Dean Street in Brooklyn. Brown was determined to do big things with the brewery. He traveled to Europe to find the "perfect" brew, found it in good old Budweis, returned home, and started brewing a beer he naturally called Budweiser. He also changed the name of the brewery to the Budweiser Brewing Co.

In the years that followed, Anheuser-Busch became less and less pleased with Brooklyn's Budweiser, especially when Brown and his cohorts began pouring considerable cash into promoting their Budweiser up the East Coast, from Brooklyn all the way to Boston. In 1898 Anheuser-

Busch brought suit. Figuring their chances of winning were pretty slim, Brown and company backed down, changed the name of the brewery to the Nassau Brewing Co., and ceased all usage of Budweiser as a trade name.

The Longest Lasting "Other Budweiser"

Far and away the longest lasting "other Budweiser" was DuBois Budweiser. First brewed by the DuBois Brewing Co., of DuBois, Pennsylvania, in 1905, it was sold in northwestern Pennsylvania until 1970, but not without numerous court battles with Anheuser-Busch. All that ended in 1970, when Judge Louis Rosenberg ruled in U.S. Supreme Court in Pittsburgh that Budweiser was the exclusive trademark of Anheuser-Busch. DuBois was forced to destroy all its DuBois Budweiser packaging by October 31 and to cease any and all future use of the name. The last "other Budweiser" was put to rest.

The year 1898 was a tough one for Brooklyn. It was merged into New York City, losing its status as America's fourth largest city, and it bid farewell to its own Budweiser.

Du Bois Budweiser: the last "other Budweiser."

KEG-BEER BRANDS:
BUDWEISER,
PILSENER,
WIENER,
ERLANGER,
CULMBACHER,
"SCHLITZ-BRÄU."

BOTTLED-BEER BRAND
PILSENER,
EXTRA-PALE,
EXTRA-STOUT,
"SCHLITZ-PORTER.

A circa 1890 Schlitz advertising piece that includes Schlitz Budweiser, thought to have been brewed for only about ten years and only in kegs. (Photo courtesy Local History Collection, Milwaukee Public Library)

Carnation "Bud" may or may not have been an attempt to capitalize on Budweiser's ever-increasing popularity. It was a product of the Franklin & Hayes Brewing Co., of Pocatello, Idaho, in business from 1904 until 1913.

The Most Amazing, Dazzling, Even Shocking "Other Budweisers"

As far back as just about anyone still alive and kicking can recall, Anheuser-Busch has been either numero uno or numero dos in beer sales — very, very largely because of Budweiser's tremendous popularity. Add to that the realization that A-B's rival for the top spot all these years has generally been Schlitz or Miller. Then take a deep breath . . . because now comes into your life the AMAZING, DAZZLING, YES, EVEN SHOCKING, FACT THAT . . .

. . . BOTH SCHLITZ AND MILLER HAVE HAD THEIR OWN BRANDS CALLED BUDWEISER. Yep, it's true. But beyond the fact that it's true, not a heck of a lot more is known. Peter Blum, historian at Stroh's, the firm that absorbed Schlitz in 1982, believes Schlitz's Budweiser to have been a not-very-important brand in Schlitz's lineup, probably brewed from the mid-1880s until perhaps the mid-1890s. A check with R. A. Horvath of the public relations department of Miller reveals little more about Miller's Budweiser. From an advertising booklet put out by Miller in the 1890s, however, we know that its Budweiser was a lot more important than was the case with Schlitz. After all, even in the oft exaggerated world of advertising copy, one couldn't have used the phrase "America's Favorite Beer" too cavalierly, could one?

Continued on next page

LEISY'S
BUDWEISER
BEER

E. J. BARTLICK
WHOLESALE DEALER
1124-1126 PENN AVE.

A Leisy's Budweiser Beer ad from the pages of an 1891 Pittsburgh directory. At the time it was most likely the primary brand of the Issac Leisy Brewing Co., a major Cleveland brewery that was to remain in operation until 1960 . . . although its brewing of a brand called Budweiser ceased before the onset of Prohibition.

11

From a booklet put out by Miller in the 1890s comes this page and the claim of their Original Milwaukee Budweiser to be "America's Favorite Beer." From the same booklet comes a bit of verse further extolling the virtues of Miller's Budweiser:

The weak, the ill, the pale and wan
Will find their strength returning,
And Miller's pure Budweiser beer
Will satisfy their yearning.

(Chorus)
Made with the famous Saazer hops,
Proclaim it from the Chimney tops,
It makes strong men of weakling fops,
And sets their souls a-burning.

An 1886 *Puck* magazine advertisement for the "Highly Celebrated" Budweis Lager, a product of Philadelphia's Prospect Brewing Co.

But Budweis beware: looming up right next to Prospect Brewery's ad—and at least four times as big—is none other than Anheuser-Busch!

But Even Anheuser-Busch Doesn't Win Them All!
In October 1983 Federal Judge Ann Aldrich ruled against Anheuser-Busch and for a Cleveland florist who'd been advertising "This Bud's for You." The judge's viewpoint: that flowers and beer are almost completely unrelated, that it would be "absurd" for anyone to confuse the two, and anyone that did was probably in serious trouble anyway.

Giuseppe Garibaldi: Patriot, Revolutionist, Soldier, Brewer

Italians aren't generally noted for their love of beer. Vino is more apt to be their cup of cheer. Yet "The Hero of Two Worlds," Giuseppe Garibaldi (1807–82), was involved with a Staten Island brewery, and the first brewery on that island to brew lager at that.

After garnering considerable fame as a revolutionary leader, Garibaldi was exiled to America in 1850. For a time he worked in a candle factory on Staten Island, but in 1852 he joined with fellow countryman Antonio Mucci (also spelled Meucci) to form the Garibaldi and Mucci Brewery. Whether Garibaldi was actually involved in the brewery or was more or less a figurehead is uncertain. What is certain, though, is that the following year, 1853, Garibaldi severed his association with the brewery, returned to Italy, and nobly aided the cause of Italian liberation.

DOES THIS MAN LOOK LIKE A BREWER? Whether or not Garibaldi was really and truly a brewer is questionable. However, the brewery with which he was involved is credited with brewing Staten Island's first lager, and it lived on long after Garibaldi's departure. Following several changes in ownership, the brewery became the Bachmann Brewing Co. and remained in operation until 1911. (Photo courtesy Culver Pictures)

Of Garibaldi the *Encyclopedia Britannica* says: "There has been no greater master of guerrilla warfare and none more successful." It does not mention his contribution to brewing.

Beer Concoctions

MMM, LIP-SMACKING GOOD. Best Figgy Sue I've ever had!

BE OF GOOD HEALTH. Wassail, from the Anglo-Saxon *wes hal*, meaning "be of good health," has long, long been a part of our Christmas tradition. It's said, in fact, that Anglo-Saxon warriors in merry old England celebrated so much from the wassail bowl that Alfred the Great, who reigned in the ninth century, attempted — unsuccessfully — to replace it in the twelve days after Christmas with abstemious and sacred observation.

As good as beer is all by itself, people have been mixing and matching it with all kinds of other things for about as long as they've been enjoying it alone.

Our forefathers — and foremothers, too — drank some wild and crazy stuff. With them, of course, such concoctions were often an important part of their heating and/or medicinal system, as well as their thirst-quenching system. Try a couple of these "oldies but goodies" and you'll see what I mean!

Tewahdiddle

½ pint (8 ounces) beer or ale
2 teaspoons brandy
½ teaspoon brown sugar
1 slice lemon
¼ teaspoon grated nutmeg

Stir the beer, brandy, and sugar together until the sugar is dissolved. Pour into glass and add slice of lemon. Grate the nutmeg over the glass. Serve hot or cold. Serves 1.

Figgy Sue

¼ pound dried figs
1 pint water
1 quart beer or ale
1 tablespoon superfine granulated sugar
pinch of ground ginger

Wash figs and simmer in water in saucepan until tender. Rub through a sieve. Heat the beer with the sugar and ginger and, when nearly boiling, add fig puree. Bring to a boil, stirring continuously. Serve hot. Serves 4.

Syllabub

½ cup seedless raisins
2 cups beer or ale
2 cups cider
1½ quarts milk
1½ teaspoons ground cinnamon
sugar to taste

Pour boiling water over raisins and let stand thirty minutes. Mix beer, cider, and milk together in a bowl. Allow to cool, then beat with a rotary beater until foamy. Pour into a punch bowl. Drain raisins and sprinkle over the mixture. Taste for sweetness, adding sugar if necessary. Sprinkle cinnamon on top. Serves 4-6.

Wassail

4 small apples
4 tablespoons brown sugar
2 cups beer or ale
¼ teaspoon ground nutmeg
½ teaspoon ground cinnamon
¼ teaspoon ground ginger
½ cup granulated sugar
1½ cups dry sherry

Peel and slice apples into rings. In a saucepan, heat the beer, nutmeg, cinnamon, ginger, sugars. and sherry. Stir until sugar is dissolved. Cook over low heat for fifteen minutes, taking care not to let the mixture boil. Pour into a punch bowl and decorate with the apple rings. Serves 6-8.

Yes, our forefathers and mothers did indeed dream up some wild and crazy beer concoctions. That's not to say, however, that the old inventive spirit isn't with us yet. A few of today's favorites might include what is called a Velvet Cup (beer and champagne) at Mory's in New Haven; Monaco, a beer and grenadine blend served at New York City's trendy Sugar Reef; Leroux 'n Brew (Leroux Peppermint Schnapps and ice-cold beer); and a reported standby at the University of Washington, Skip and Go Naked Punch (beer, vodka, and lemonade). Our forefathers and mothers would undoubtedly be impressed!

Note: For the "oldies but goodies" concoctions, I am indebted to Carole Fahy's excellent book, *Cooking with Beer* (Dover Publications, New York, 1978). The newer beer and something-else blendings are gleaned from Emanuel Greenberg's "To the Tables Down at Mory's . . ." in the March 1983 issue of *Playboy*.

Names Will Never Hurt Me

Scofflaw: the word brings to mind — my mind, anyway — visions of a person with a string of parking or traffic violations left unpaid. Worse yet, I picture the poor soul's car being towed away as a consequence of nonpayment, as a consequence of being a scofflaw!

But the word has its origins, not in parking or traffic, but in beer and booze.

By 1923 the officials responsible for prohibition enforcement were becoming increasingly aghast at its lack of enforcement. The prohibition law was the Rodney Dangerfield of its day: it got no respect. Officials thought it would help to come up with a word, a new word, to stamp offenders, a strong word, a word to make people cringe.

A Massachusetts millionnaire and staunch prohibitionist by the name of Delcevare King agreed and sponsored a contest to find the best word. The winner was to get only two hundred dollars, but over twenty-five thousand entries came pouring in. The winning word, announced by King in January 1924, was amazingly coined by two different people. The word was, of course, *scofflaw*. Cringe.

"I have a total irreverence for anything connected with society, except that which makes the road safer, the beer stronger, the old men and women warmer in the winter and happier in the summer."

—*Brendan Behan*

You Don't Have to Drink Beer to Be a Fatso

Everybody knows him: the guy with the "beer belly" that hasn't touched a drop of beer since 1969. Or the woman with the telephone pole legs that aren't caused by beer, as folks assume, but by a fondness for chocolate nougat and fettucine alfredo and french fries and double-dip ice cream cones and . . . just plain lack of exercise.

Here's an exercise in the joy of calorie counting:

one ounce of chablis . . . . 22 calories
one ounce of champagne . . . . 25 calories
one ounce of soave . . . . 27 calories

BEER AND THE BELLY. Beer gets a bummer rap than it should when it comes to being fat.

WHO SEZ I CAN'T HOLD MY BEER?!

THERE'S A GRAND AND GLORIOUS FEELING PASSING ONE TUB TO ANOTHER

FROM OUT OF ONE BARREL INTO ANOTHER!

I'M GOING TO QUENCH MY THIRST EVEN IF I BURST!

Circa 1950 postcard art

one ounce of dry sherry . . . . 36 calories
one ounce of Campari . . . . . . 47 calories
one ounce of distilled spirits,
    80 proof . . . . 65 calories
one ounce of distilled spirits,
    90 proof . . . . 75 calories
one ounce of amaretto . . . . . . 80 calories
one ounce of distilled spirits,
    100 proof . . . . 85 calories
one ounce of Tia Maria . . . . . 92 calories
one ounce of Drambuie . . . . . 110 calories

. . . versus the joy of very few calories to count:

one ounce of lite/light beer . . 8 calories
one ounce of regular beer . . . 13 calories

OUNCE FOR OUNCE, BEER IS THE LEAST FATTENING ALCOHOLIC BEVERAGE IN THE WORLD!

And beer stacks up very nicely against almost any nonalcoholic goody you can think of, too.

one ounce of a Baby Ruth . . . 135 calories
one ounce of Fritos . . . . 155 calories
one ounce of potato chips . . . 160 calories
one average portion of chili . . 448 calories
one Friendly's chocolate Fribble . . . . 470 calories
one Dairy Queen banana split . . . . . . 540 calories
one McDonald's Big Mac . . . . 541 calories
one Gino's fish platter . . . . . . 650 calories
one Burger King Whopper . . 650 calories
and especially for you Chinese enthusiasts:
one average portion of chicken and
    cashews . . . . 750 calories
one average portion of sweet and sour
    chicken . . . . 1,150 calories

Dietetically Non-Fattening

It all makes beer look darned good, doesn't it? Government rules and regulations, however, have made it difficult for brewers to take advantage of beer's relatively non-fattening qualities. You just can't stand up and shout: "Hey, our beer will make you a slimbo!"

One brewer came very close to doing just

that, though. They plastered California newspapers and billboards with the message that their beer was "Dietetically Non-Fattening." The brewer was the California Brewing Association, of San Francisco and Los Angeles, brewers of Acme Beer. Actually the brewery's first slogan, begun in 1934, was "Non-Fattening Refreshment," but this was changed to the "Dietetically Non-Fattening" line by 1936. Acme's advertising copy explained it all:

> Tests show that it [Acme Beer] contains less than 25% of the fattening substances that are in most of the non-alcoholic beverages, and that the carbohydrates contained in Acme Beer are fully fermented and therefore are non-fattening.

Sound like mumbo jumbo? Well maybe yes, but maybe no. Acme's brewmaster, Anton Dolenz — fondly referred to in the industry as "The Old Master" — *had* perfected the formula for a lighter, drier beer during Prohibition, so the claim was not without its merits.

"Dietetically Non-Fattening" held up under FTC scrutiny in 1936 . . . and was used by the brewery as its major theme on and off for the next fifteen or so years. At that point the FTC again got into the act. In April 1951 the commission ruled that, yes, "Beer in itself is for all practical purposes a non-fattening beverage, for the reason that it is a food beverage with a relatively low calorie content." However, added the commission in its wisdom, Acme's use of "Non-Fattening" as a slogan is deceptive. In all future advertising, the slogan had to be accompanied clearly and closely by the qualifying statement: "when taken in substitution for foods of equal or greater calorie value and not in addition to the normally required diet." In other words, beer is nonfattening as long as it is enjoyed in lieu of something else equally fattening or nonfattening.

The brewery's response? It stepped up the use of its other primary slogan, in use since mid-1949 . . . "The New Acme: Slow-brewed for Fine Flavor."

ON THE ROAD AGAIN. A prolific billboard advertiser, Acme had over a thousand boards in California alone in 1940, many of which — as here — featured the shapely "girlie" art of George Petty. (Photo courtesy Foster & Kleiser, Los Angeles)

DIETETICALLY NON-FATTENING. Looking slim and refreshed, too, is this late 1930s lovely lady . . . all thanks to Acme and its dietetically non-fattening beer.

1934 — NON FATTENING ACME BEER

Superlatives: Where Are They Now?

So what do you do when you can't think of anything too awfully original to say about something? Well there's always the old superlative bag. It's easy to dip in and come out with the likes of "The Best," "The Finest," "The Highest." And copywriters have been doing just that for years ... to sell beer as well as soap, washing machines, and just about everything else.

Ah, but does it work? Are superlatives *the best* way to sell *the highest* amount of even *the finest* beer? Maybe yes, maybe no ... these brewers thought so.

In the not-always-too-imaginative race for superlatives, we've had ...
- the same "Best"
- back to back "Bests"
- and even a brand that was flat out named "The Finest."

"Finest Beer Brewed." 1904 ad for Moerlein's, a product of the Christian Moerlein Brewing Co., Cincinnati, 1866-1919. (Note: Christian Moerlein is presently being used by the Hudepohl-Schoenling Brewing Co. as the name for its highly regarded Cincinnati Select Beer ... and they'd undoubtedly still consider it the "Finest Beer Brewed.")

"Still the Best" was a slogan used by both the Hedrick Brewing Co. of Albany, New York, 1891-1965, and the Horlacher Brewing Co. of Allentown, Pennsylvania, 1902-1978, for many years.

"Connecticut's Best"
Cremo Brewing Co., New Britain, Connecticut, 1905-1955

18

"Buffalo's Best"
Magnus Beck Brewing Co., Buffalo, 1860-1955

"Best at any Time"
Clock Ale, Waterbury Brewing Company, Waterbury, Conn., 1934-1938

"The Best What Is!"
Norwich Brewing Co., Norwich, New York, 1904–1915

Serving only the best at Al's Beer Parlor, Mankato, Minnesota, circa 1950

"The Finest Beer in Town"
Duquesne Brewing Co., Pittsburgh, 1899–1972 (Duquesne name still used by C. Schmidt & Sons)

"Best Beer Brewed"
Beverwyck Brewing Co., Albany, New York, 1893–1950

Did it live up to its name? Was "The Finest" really the finest? Well only the folks living in or around Bay City in the years 1933 through 1943 — when "The Finest" was brewed — really know for sure. The next time you're up that way, it might be fun to track down an old-timer... and ask.

Continued on next page

Superlatives, Continued

"Best Beer Ever Brewed" versus "The Best Brews in the World." Both ads are from a 1956 Boston Red Sox program and were but a page apart.

"The Best Lager Beer on this Coast" versus "The Best Beer on Earth." Both ads ran in the 1898 "Blue and Gold," the University of California yearbook, and, again, were but one page part.

The Battle of Troy . . . early Twentieth-Century style Stoll Brewing Co., 1895–1920 Isengart Brewing Co., 1901–1915

20

There's Old...

You'd be wise not to hold your breath while waiting for Ford, Chrysler, or GM to come out with a car called the Old Michigan. Don't watch for Gillette to change its deodorant's name from Right Guard to Old Guard. And you're probably not about to hear McDonald's say "The heck with the Big Mac ... from now on we're selling Old Heidelbergers!" Yet all of these names — Old Michigan, Old Guard, and Old Heidelberger — have been used as beer names in the not very distant past, along with Old Bacchus, Old Baron, Old Broadway, Old Joe, Old Maltster, Old Rip, Old Rogue, Old Schleisingerville, etc., etc., etc.

All told, from Old Abbey to Old Ypsilanti there have been over 165 "Olds" sold by the brewers of America since repeal, including some that have been less than fully thirst provoking: Old Anchor, Old Dobbin, Old Gross, Old Hilltop, Old Mule, and Old Scout among them.

Although this stress on oldness rather than newness may appear strange, there are two good reasons for it: beer is a product that has (a) traditionally prided itself on being properly aged and (b) in having been able to withstand the test of time.

So ... don't be surprised if someday soon you're in your favorite delicatessen, supermarket, or package store and you find yourself face to face with Old Ronald, Old Graffiti, Old Subway, or, if this writer hangs in there long enough, Old Anderson.

And There's Old...

Here's a still-waiting-to-be-opened bottle of beer that really and truly does deserve to be called "Old." It's from the former Adam Scheidt Brewing Co., of Norristown, Pennsylvania, and dates back to about the time William McKinley was shot. Actually at this point it should be called "stuff" rather than "beer." Drink it and you know you'd be drinking something different!

Yankee Stadium: The House That ~~Ruth~~ Ruppert Built

Jacob Ruppert, 1867–1939

A heavy hitter in political, social, and sporting circles, Jacob Ruppert was even more successful in business. He held substantial real estate holdings, was president of the U.S. Brewers Association for sixteen years, and was fully at the helm of Jacob Ruppert, Inc., one of the East's most dominant brewing forces. (Photo courtesy New York Yankees)

Jacob Ruppert, Inc. as it looked in an artist's 1933 stylized view. The brewery folded in 1965. Today the site — between Second and Third Avenues in the low nineties — is occupied by Ruppert-Yorkville Towers, a huge high-rise housing complex.

"I remember Babe Ruth when he used to come up to get his salary increase. Then you'd have a whole crowd waiting on Third Avenue between Ninety-first and Ninety-second Streets. That was the brewery office, in the middle of the block. Then there'd be big headlines the next day: "Babe Ruth Gets Another Raise!"
— Ed Sexton, lifelong resident of the Yorkville area of Manhattan

No athletic team — anytime, anyplace — has ever so dominated the sports scene the way the New York Yankees have dominated baseball in this century. You may love them for it; you may hate them for it. Regardless, you have one man to thank or to blame: Jacob Ruppert.

Jacob Ruppert — known as "The Colonel" to all his many friends and associates — was quite a guy. Born in 1867, he was an extremely successful brewer and powerful man about town in New York City commercial, political, and social circles. His yacht, the Albatross, was a familiar sight on Long Island Sound. He was a member of the Atlantic, the New York, and the Larchmont yacht clubs. And just in case he had any free time, he belonged to the New York Athletic Club, the Lambs, the Manhattan Club, and the Arion and Liederkranz societies. He was an almost insatiable collector . . . of jade, porcelain, bronzes, fine art, rare books and bindings, yachts, race horses, Indian artifacts, and just for good measure, monkeys. He bred and sometimes raced prize harness horses, and he bred prize St. Bernards. His personal favorite was named Oh Boy. The Colonel considered him to be the finest St. Bernard ever sired.

Ruppert was also active in politics, representing his district as congressman for three terms. He was one of the principal backers of Admiral Richard E. Byrd's second Antarctic expedition, so principal that the ex-

pedition's flagship was named the Jacob Ruppert . . . and 1,200 cases of Ruppert Beer were packed aboard in case the fifty-six-man force got thirsty.

And, of course, the Colonel was a colonel . . . in the New York National Guard.

But it was his involvement with the Yankees that earned Ruppert his greatest fame. The funny thing was that he was a rabid Giant fan; had been since he was a kid. He was enamored of "Muggsie" McGraw and his team of true Giants: Christy Mathewson, Rube Marquard, Laughing Larry Doyle, Freddie Snodgrass, et al. He had little use for the upstart American League, even less for the Yankees and their losing ways. Since joining the league in 1903, the Yankees had no pennants and eight second-division finishes to show through 1914. They'd finished in the cellar or next to it in 1912, 1913, and 1914. Inept they were. Still Ruppert loved the game and, finding the Giants not for sale, lowered his sights and, with partner Cap Huston, purchased the Yankees in January of 1915. The purchase price was $460,000 . . . less than a good — or not so good — reserve infielder earns nowadays.

Ruppert did nothing halfheartedly. When he bought the Yankees, they became his baby. He poured enthusiasm — and money — into the team. It was he who began what has since become a Yankee trademark, the buying of stars from other teams. Actually

JACOB RUPPERT'S BREWERY
THIRD AVE., NEW YORK

"The thing I remember mostly about the Ruppert Brewery was Colonel Ruppert really ran the place. He was in complete charge. He was there every day in the office. He had his finger on every part of the development and the sale of that beer. He was a tough guy: he ran the brewery the way he wanted it run."
— Stan Lomax, one of the deans of American sportscasting and the host of the Stan Lomax Sports Report ("This Is Stan Lomax, Your Ruppert Sports Reporter") for the better part of a decade in the late 1930s and early 1940s.

Ruppert went a step further than any of his successors: he bought (plundered is the term they used in Boston!) almost the entire Red Sox team from Harry Frazee, the debt-ridden Broadway producer who owned the Boston franchise. From the Sox came much of the nucleus of the Yankees' success all through the 1920s: Babe Ruth (for $100,000 plus a $300,000 personal loan), Carl Mays, Jumping Joe Dugan, Duffy Lewis, Herb Pennock, George Pipgras, Bullet Joe Bush, Everett Scott, and "The Brooklyn Schoolboy," Waite Hoyt.

The year 1921 was a major one for Ruppert. He bought out Cap Huston's half share, becoming sole owner. And the Yankees won their first-ever pennant . . . the beginning of a skein of ten flags and seven world championships they would win over the twenty-four years the Colonel owned the team.

By 1921 Yankee Stadium was also in the works. The Yankees had been sharing the Polo Grounds through the generosity of the Giants. But a rivalry was developing between the two clubs for the favor of New York fans, and the Yankees were asked to think about leaving.

Ruppert's reaction was to construct the most magnificent baseball palace in America. And perhaps to rub it into the "Jints," the site the Colonel selected was directly across the Harlem River from the Polo Grounds. As was his trademark, the construction of his new ball park was not done in the least halfheartedly. No expense was spared. No corner was cut. Yankee Stadium — officially opened to a record crowd of close to sixty thousand on April 18, 1923 — was the result. It should have been called Ruppert Stadium.

Yankee Stadium today. Behind center field there are plaques honoring the great names of the Yankees' past. One of those plaques is of Jacob Ruppert. (Photo courtesy New York Yankees)

Yankee Stadium, Opening Day, April 18, 1923

They all came to see what the Colonel had built. (Photo courtesy New York Yankees)

"My idea of a good ballgame is one where the Yankees have a thirteen-run lead in the top of the ninth with two out and two strikes on the hitter."

— Jacob Ruppert

23

Tribute to a Breweriana Pioneer

Ernie Oest looking blustery.

Ernie Oest looking happy.

As you've hopefully noticed, goodly chunks of *From Beer to Eternity* are tongue in cheek. This is a section, though, that is not. It's an unabashed tribute to a somewhat blustery but quite wonderful guy by the name of Ernie Oest, "Uncle" Ernie of Port Jefferson Station, New York.

Uncle Ernie was one of the very real pioneers in this "business" of giving a damn not just about the beer, but also about preserving for posterity the accoutrements of the beer: the package in which it was dressed, the brewery from whence it flowed, the memories and stories that enhanced it.

Starting back in 1930 — before half the folks in this country today were even born — he began soaking labels off near beer bottles and putting them in scrapbooks. The return of real beer in 1933 added, of course, that much more fuel to Ernie's fire. The collection grew by leaps and bounds.

It was Ernie's eventual decision to go right to the source, however, that especially stamped him as a man of distinction. As he tells it:

Starting about 1948, every time I had a vacation I would go on a beer tour.

It's like any other hobby or collection: you went to where the source was. So if you're looking for beer items, you went to where they were made, where they were available. And I sure as heck wanted to drink their beer. And to add to my collection — to get their labels, or their signs, or their bottles. And to take pictures of their brewery. Maybe this brewery was a little more picturesque; maybe their beer was a little more interesting; maybe their label was more attractive and harder to get. It was always an adventure . . . what's in the next town?

There's a million stories. I almost got killed a couple of times. I remember up in the Harvard Brewery in Lowell, Massachusetts, dogs cornered me. But I was lucky: they were trained to hold, not attack. So the watchman came and I told him what I wanted. he said, "Help yourself."

Those were the days when every brewmaster wanted to have a distinguishable brew. In other words, you could tell his beer was different than the others. He had his own taste, not identical like today, where they all taste alike.

I'll tell you one thing about the beer business: I've yet to be in a brewery where the guys makin' it didn't drink it!

I fell out of some breweries. The best was the Matz Brewery in Bellaire, Ohio. It was only a little thing. Well, I went in the office and told 'em my hobby. "Oh, come right in," they said. In them days the collectors hadn't worn out the mat. Now most of them thought I wanted beer. I said what I wanted was a tray and some labels. "Oh, have a beer," they said. They had a big mural in the hospitality room, a big mural of the town. When the pressed a button, certain windows lit up and if you looked close you could see certain risque scenes. It was a beautiful mural!

Now this was only about ten in the morning, but they said, "Oh, you gotta test this. This is the brewmaster's special. And you gotta drink this one. This is the brewmaster's special."

Well, I fell outta there at ten-thirty in the morning and I couldn't go no further. I was licked.

When Ernie wasn't falling out of breweries, he was taking photos of them. Following are but a very few of the brewhouses captured by Ernie's golden camera, with commentary by me.

The Fountain Brewing Co., closed in 1965, was built into a bluff overlooking the mighty

Blackhawk Brewing Co., Davenport, Iowa, 1948

Northampton Brewery Corp., Northampton, Pennsylvania, 1954

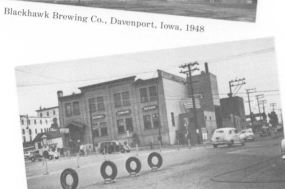

Greenway's, Inc., Syracuse, New York, 1949

Fountain Brewing Co., Fountain City, Wisconsin, circa 1951

Sunshine Brewing Co., Reading, Pennsylvania, 1956

Gluek Brewing Co., Minneapolis, circa 1952

Storck Brewing Co., Slinger, Wisconsin, circa 1959

Continued on next page

Mississippi. Sad to say, its site today is occupied by a most unattractive-looking apartment complex.

Gluek's produced one of America's earliest malt liquors. Its Gluek's Stite was put on the market way back in 1943.

Topper Ale and Beer were favorites throughout western New York through 1970, when Standard-Rochester shut down.

Berlin Country Club Beer was one of several brands put out by the Berlin Brewing Co. As with all the other breweries captured here by Ernie's camera, it is now out of business. Its last year of operation was 1964.

If the Cleveland-Sandusky Brewing Co. appears to be tipping somewhat, it's in tribute to Uncle Ernie Oest, a breweriana buff long before anyone else even thought of coining the word.

Berlin Brewing Co., Berlin, Wisconsin, 1959

Cleveland-Sandusky Brewing Co., Cleveland, 1960

Standard-Rochester Brewing Co., Rochester, 1958

Matz Brewing Co., Bellaire, Ohio, circa 1950

Mountain Brewing Co., Roanoke, Virginia, 1958

Mixed Up, Muddled Up

It's a mixed-up, muddled-up shook-up world.
— *"Lola," the Kinks, 1970*

The Kinks weren't just whistlin' Dixie. There're a lot of things in this old world that are, indeed, somewhat on the mixed-up side. The wonderful world of beer signs is no exception. Here for your viewing pleasure is . . .

The Lage Bee Sign,
New York City, January 1983

The Upside-down Sign,
Chicago, August 1985

The Half a Sign,
Winona, Minnesota, October 1984

There's a pretty fair excuse for the chewed-off Geo. Ehret wall painting: they've been out of business for over thirty-five years, with this particular sign appearing to predate Prohibition. But Heileman and Miller?

One can only wonder if Miller's found truth to the age-old adage: "Half a sign is better than none." Meanwhile, keep ever on the alert as you wend your way around your own neighborhood. Who knows what mixed-up, muddled-up, shook-up beer advertising specimens *you* might find.

27

Going to the Dogs

B eer and our canine friends would not appear to have much in common. Oh sure, some dogs like beer. And they're both good friends of man (and woman, too), but that's about it. So it is somewhat surprising to see the number of brewers that've made use of Fido in their advertising.

Here are a few examples that I think you'll like.

TO THE RESCUE. A mighty rare specimen of breweriana is this solid brass St. Bernard clock, which was given away gratis to favored accounts in the 1890s. The Highland Brewing Co., in fact, existed only in the 1890s. It was in business only from 1894 to 1899.

"SAY OLD READING BEER." Somehow I don't think our four-footed friend here is going to say "Old Reading Beer." Maybe the brewery should've changed its brand name to Woof.

YOU LUCKY DOG. This has always been a personal favorite of mine...just a happy-as-can-be pooch and his beer and cigar. The brewing plant of the former Lembeck & Betz Brewing Co. (1869-1920) in Jersey City still remains intact, very close to the entrance to the Holland Tunnel. It is in the process of being converted into luxury condominiums.

BULLDOG BRAND. There have also been numerous brands named bulldog. Here's the Old Bulldog himself, Jack Dempsey, endorsing one of them, as well he should...he was a sizable stockholder in the brewery—Acme Breweries, of San Francisco and Los Angeles—that put it out. (Photo courtesy David "Santa" Williams)

THE DOGGONE GOOD BEER. Possibly the best use of "dog advertising" was put forth by the Frankenmuth Brewing Co. of Frankenmuth, Michigan. Their sales mascot was a dachshund named, most aptly, Frankie. Clever enough; but what was even more clever was extending the dog theme into nicknaming their brewery "the Home of the Doggone Good Beer."

LINED UP. Old Frankenmuth Lager trucks lined up outside the brewery, 1937. (Photo courtesy Mack Museum)

"WATCHDOG OF QUALITY." Providence's James Hanley Brewing Co. utilized a bulldog as their "Watchdog of Quality" symbol from 1913 right down to the sad day when they closed their doors in 1957. In fact, they thought so highly of the bulldog that they even had the original portrait of him insured with Lloyds of London.

Although Frankie, Hanley's "Watchdog of Quality," and other legendary beer dogs of the past have been retired to the canine hall of fame, beer/dog advertising does reappear from time to time. The most recent example that comes to mind is Stroh's use of the unseen — but definitely present — Alex in their 1984–85 Stroh Beer Lovers television campaign. Who can forget the classic: "Alex, that better be your water!"

Where Were You in 1829? An Interview with Dick Yuengling

Nestled high on a hill among the many hills of Pottsville, Pennsylvania, stands D. G. Yuengling & Son ... which could, to prove a point, more rightfully be called D. G. Yuengling & Son & Grandson & Great-grandson & Great-great Grandson. The point: Yuengling's has been around a long, long time ... long enough to be America's oldest brewery.

Chances are that you weren't in Pottsville in 1829, but if you had been you could have helped recently arrived German emigrant David G. Yuengling found his brewery, and you could have enjoyed his beer.

Chances are that you weren't in Pottsville in 1986 or 1987 either, so we've gone for you. We talked with fifth-generation president Dick Yuengling in his timeless office at the brewery. And we enjoyed his beer.

Dick how does it feel to be the newly annointed president of America's oldest brewery?
Well I'm very honored to be in the sense that there's so few breweries left in the

A JOB TO DO. "I feel I have a job to do to keep the place going."

country. In *Brewer's Digest* there's thirty. That's all that's left. And we're the nineteenth largest brewery in the country at this point.

It's also special to be president of not just a brewery but the oldest. It's something that I've always wanted to do. I started work here when I was fifteen and I feel I have a job to do to keep the place going. I enjoy it. I enjoy the business.

What thoughts have you about any different future brews to go along with your Yuengling's Beer, your Lord Chesterfield Ale, and your celebrated Pottsville Porter?
We found that the light beer market is becoming such a big percentage of the sales in this country that we're going to have to get into that. What we're trying to accomplish is to maintain the great percentage of this local market that we've attained through the people being loyal to us here. We probably have 40 to 45 percent of the business in Pottsville and Schuylkill County. How long can you maintain that, being a

FROM ALL OVER THE COUNTRY. "We had about four thousand visitors last year. They've been here from all over the country."

30

brewery of our size? And the light beers are digging into us a little bit. This isn't a big light beer area, but it's becoming that. People are more worried about their weight and the drinking laws. They drink light beer when they go out. To maintain that percentage of the market we have to get into a light beer.

The local market, then, is essential to your success?
Oh there's no question about it. They keep us alive. If it weren't for that we wouldn't be here.

So you don't see anything more exotic than a light beer?
Yeah, I do. This [the light beer] will give us four brews, and the brewmaster's going to have his hands full with this on account of the size of our plant. And we are operating at 80 percent of capacity. Where do we put this stuff? So what we are kicking around in the near future is more or less a premium-priced blend of our ale and porter. We don't even know what we're going to call it yet. I see it at this point, probably, coming out the end of the summer, maybe in the fall [of 1986].

Do you ever think back and wonder how your great, great grandfather, the man who founded the brewery, would feel about the beers you brew today and the brewery as it is? Is he observing you from up above, do you think?
I've thought of that and my answer is that I think he must be very proud that it's still going. I know if my great, great grandson was runnin' the place, I'd be happy about it, be very proud. It's something nobody else in the country has accomplished in this industry.

How well do you do with your ale and your porter?
The ale has taken off in sales fantastically. Between the ale and the porter we account for about 15 percent of our total sales, with a little better than half of the 15 percent being ale.

HE MUST BE VERY PROUD. "I've thought of that and my answer to that is I think he (brewery founder David G. Yuengling, pictured here in portrait form) must be very proud that it's still going."

You probably do better with your ale and porter shipping it away from this area, don't you?
It's funny, in certain areas the ale sells better and we don't sell porter, and in some areas it's the reverse. You get down into Maryland, for some reason, and the porter goes very well. Washington, they do a nice job with the porter.

The Philadelphia market does very well with the ale and so does the New York market. Not New York City, in upstate New York: Binghamton across the Pennsylvania border, over to Port Jervis, New York.

Of the three products you brew now, which is your favorite?
I wouldn't pick a favorite. It depends on everybody's taste. I think our porter is good because it has the proper characteristics that a porter should. Our ale certainly does and our sales justify that. And our beer's been selling well.

As far as taste goes, I like our beer. That's what I drink. I'll sit down and drink one or two bottles of porter, that's enough. And ale, I'm not a nut on ale, but if I were, I'd drink ours.

Continued on next page

31

THEY KEEP US ALIVE. "We probably have 40 to 45 percent of the business in Pottsville and Schuylkill County. They keep us alive. If it weren't for that we wouldn't be here."

Billboard above route 61, the major road into Pottsville

I have four daughters! We'll have a girl runnin' this place maybe someday. They're seven through fourteen.

Have any of them expressed any interest in the brewery?
At that age they don't know which way they're going. I told my oldest daughter —her name is Jennifer—that this year she can start work. I said, "Do you want to?" and she said, "Yeah." So she'll be fifteen in June. I said, "You know I started when I was fifteen."

What percentage of your beer sales is draft?
About 30 percent. It's high. It's been goin' up. Last year we had a 6 percent increase, and so far this year our draft is up. In fact we've just modernized, I would say, our

Would you say your brewery has reached a cult status among beer lovers?
I don't think it's reached that. I think it could, marketed properly. But I don't know how much beer cults drink, if you know what I mean. I don't know if a brewery this size can survive on a cult status. I think our ale and porter could contribute greatly to the profitability of this plant, but I don't think that the word *cult* as they use the term, that this brewery could survive on the business that could be derived from that.

Do you give tours of the brewery?
Yes, we have tours twice a day, 10:00 in the morning and 1:30 in the afternoon, Monday through Thursday. We don't have anything on Friday. We had about four thousand visitors last year. It's nice. I couldn't fathom that number of people coming to go through this place. They've been here from all over the country. One Friday afternoon a fellow and his wife came in here from Alaska.

As I recollect, you have a daughter or two . . . but no sons.
I guess I've been busy since you last heard.

GIBBSVILLE. Pottsville was also the home of John O'Hara (1905-70), one of America's most prolific writers (*From the Terrace, Butterfield 8, Pal Joey, A Rage to Live, Ten North Frederick,* numerous others). The Gibbsville of many of his stories and novels was a thinly veiled Pottsville . . . and the importance of beer and brewing to the region no stranger to his writing. O'Hara lived a literal stone's throw from Yuengling's, shown here in the background.

YUENGLING'S EIN CUTÉ BIER.
Interviewing brewery presidents
can provoke a hefty thirst, so before
poking around Pottsville, a jewel of
a smallish eastern Pennsylvania city,
I stopped in at Heinbach's Bar,
down the hill from the brewery. A
good-sized draft (Yuengling's, of
course!) was twenty-five cents, the
four or five customers conversed as
fluently in German as in English,
and bartender/proprietor Bill Heinbach had nothing but kind words to
say about the brewery ("They take
good care of us") and their product
("We certainly do sell a lot of
Yuengling's, far more than any other
brand."). Concluded Bill, in German,
"Yuengling's ein cuté bier" . . .
Yuengling's is good beer.

RUSTING AND ROTTING. Up
until recently Pottsville had a
second brewery, too. The Mount
Carbon Brewery, brewers of
Bavarian Beer, stood at the
southern edge of the city. Alas,
Mount Carbon closed in 1976
and has since been torn down,
replaced with a seafood market
and a pizzeria. About all that
remains of over 130 years of
brewing are these truck bod-
ies, rusting and rotting up the
hill a block or so from the
former brewery site.

draft operation. We palletized it, which to
us it was a big deal because they were
rolling kegs around here for 156 years.

*To what do you attribute the increase in
draft sales?*
I attribute it to the loyalty of the local
people, because it's all done locally.

*Yes, but weren't they loyal ten years ago,
too?*
Well, they were just becomin' loyal, not ten
years ago, about seven years ago. When we
hit our one hundred fiftieth anniversary
here in 1979 is when our beer really started
to sell locally. The local people saw it [the
anniversary celebration] on television, "PM
Magazine." They saw it, too, I think on "60
Minutes." It was shows like these that did
five- to ten-minute segments on us, and the
local people saw that and said, "Hey, we
got something here in Pottsville, in Schuylkill
County, that's known nationally now." And

they just kinda got behind our product. It
was neat. You gotta give the people all the
credit in the world.

*Dick, thanks very much. Let's hope
Yuengling's is still sitting here on the side
of this hill brewing good beer, ale, and
porter for at least another 157 years.*
I'm glad you came in, Will. It's always a
pleasure.

Mayor Knows Best

"Just relax, stay inside and open
a six-pack."
— *Buffalo mayor James Griffin
on what to do during the heavy snow
season on the Niagara Frontier,
December 1985*

Beer Flowed Like Beer: New Beer's Eve/New Beer's Day

ROLL OUT THE BARRELS. While only twenty states became legally wet on April 7, most of the remaining twenty-eight soon followed suit. Here are the first barrels being rolled out in Providence, Rhode Island, on April 10. (Photo courtesy *The Providence Journal-Bulletin*)

The biggest day in American beerdom's long, illustrious, and oh so wonderfully thirst-quenching history was without a doubt New Beer's Eve/New Beer's Day, April 6/April 7, 1933. After a thirteen-year hiatus, legal beer bounced back on the scene . . . and the better part of America hollered and whooped it up like crazy.

At one minute past the stroke of midnight, April 6, beer was kosher again in twenty states and the District of Columbia. It was part of FDR's plan for a return to prosperity . . . and America loved it. Beer flowed like beer in restaurants, make-shift bars, home parties . . . but mostly in the streets. Throngs surrounded breweries in cities and towns and cheered themselves hoarse as the triumphant moment approached when delivery trucks would once again roll. Downtowns were bedlam. It was like New Year's Eve, St. Patrick's Day, and the Fourth of July all rolled into one.

NEAR BEER IS DEAD. Midtown Manhattan was packed with thousands of New Yorkers who turned out to help bury near beer the night of April 6. Here's a small part of the jubilant throng at Times Square . . . (Photo courtesy *New York News*)

San Francisco reported thousands scrambling gleefully around the city's three back-in-operation breweries; in Milwaukee, over 100,000 friends of beer slapped each other on the back, dancing and singing "Happy Days Are Here Again"; President Roosevelt was toasted long and late in the hotels, restaurants, and rathskellers of St. Paul; and "The Sage of Baltimore," H. L. Menken, naturally enough got in the act down Maryland-way. Partaking of the new brew, he proclaimed: "Pretty good . . . not bad at all."

Beer was described as "flowing freely and in great volume" in Philadelphia . . . but, then again, those exact same words could have been used to describe just about every locale where beer was legalized; America consumed over 1,000,000 barrels of the amber liquid on New Beer's Day. That foams out to over 1,300,000 gallons — or 2,323,000 six-packs — per *hour*!

But perhaps closer to home, closer to the heart is a story still fondly recalled by Father Cosgrove of St. Ignatius Loyola Roman Catholic Church, Park Avenue and Eighty-fourth Street, New York City.

I remember, when I was a student at Fordham University, there was a man who taught mathematics, a no-nonsense individual. We could never get this guy to smile. No amount of practical jokes could ever get a rise out of this man.

So the first day beer was again on sale, we decided that we would all go off campus for lunch and each one of us would come back with two bottles of beer under his jacket. Then, when we all came back before the period began, we filled his desk with beer.

So the old gentleman comes in for his mathematics period, looks at this desk . . . and we saw the first smile for years. And he smiled for many weeks thereafter, too.

The generally sour old math prof was not alone. In the hours and days after New Beer's Eve, much of America was right there smiling along with him.

. . . while Jack Dempsey and Jimmy "Schnozzola" Durante get set to tap the first keg at Broadway's Paradise Restaurant. (Photo courtesy *Baltimore News-American*)

The Care and Feeding of Beer Glasses

Let's face it, if you like beer, you like beer. It tastes good out of anything . . . right out of a bottle or can, right out of a paper cup or coffee cup. Heck, it even tastes good out of an egg cup. Ah, but think how much better it tastes when it's drunk out of a proper beer glass, and a proper beer glass that's been cared for properly.

There are six or so major types of beer glasses, as illustrated below. My own favorite is the thin-lipped, straight-sided model known as a shell, which is pictured on the extreme left. But there are days when a brew will taste better out of a schooner or the pint glass or, very occasionally, even the mug or pilsener glass.

Regardless of your particular choice, any glass will serve you — and your beer — better if it's properly cared for. Here are the basics:

1. Use your beer glass(es) strictly for beer, ale, porter, stout; never for soda, milk, iced tea, or other such nonbeery substances. Beer is an extremely sensitive beverage that reacts poorly with *anything* else, and no matter how well you feel

DON'T LET YOUR BEER GLASSES GET YOU DOWN. Care for your beer glasses . . . and they'll care for you.

you've washed your glass, chances are there's still a residue of sarsaparilla or milk or whatever to befoul the full flavor of your brew.

2. Do not wash your beer glass(es) with soap or detergent of any kind. Use a solution of salt or baking soda and very hot water; then rinse with clean, very hot water. Sponges and dishcloths should be avoided.

3. Allow your glass(es) to air dry. Do not dry them with a paper towel or a dishtowel.

PICK YOUR GLASS. From left to right: shell, hour glass (with or without the "Harp Lager Beer"), mug (compliments of Plank's Bier Garten, Columbus, Ohio), pint glass (which should really only be brimming with stout or hearty ale!), schooner, pilsener (this one advertises Edelbrau, a Brooklyn beer that last saw the inside of a glass — any glass — in 1946).

The World's Largest Six-pack

PROPER VERSUS IMPROPER. This man's beer glass has been cared for properly...

...This man's beer glass hasn't been.

CHEERS. Cheers to you; cheers to your beer; cheers to your beer glass!

In LaCrosse, Wisconsin, close by the banks of the Mississippi, stands "The World's Largest Six-pack." It's Heileman's Old Style waiting to be canned or bottled in more traditional fashion. The six giant cans hold 22,200 barrels of beer, enough to fill 7,340,796 cans. Placed end to end that number of cans would stretch out for 565 miles and would provide a person with a six-pack a day for 3,351 years.

Any way you measure it, it's one heck of a lot of Old Style!

113,000 GALLONS. This is the front three of the giant cans that make up "The World's Largest Six-pack." Each can holds over 113,000 gallons of sparkling lager!

Milwaukee: The City That Made Beer Famous

Milwaukee ... the very mention of the Wisconsin metropolis is enough to send thirst buds up and down the throat, with visions of a seemingly endless parade of frosty, foamy mugs popping into mind. Even people that have never before enjoyed a brew in their life have been known to develop desire-for-beer-itis upon nearing Milwaukee!

But why Milwaukee? Why is it Milwaukee that became synonymous with beer in America? Why not Des Moines or Boston or Cleveland? Or for that matter, Chicago or Denver or Omaha?

Had to Hustle a Little Harder

Milwaukee was settled in 1818, but it wasn't settled by a brewer. It wasn't even settled by a German. The first permanent settler was Solomon Laurent Juneau, a French-Canadian agent for Astor's American Fur Company. Juneau's settlement joined to-

gether with several other area settlements in 1835 to form Milwaukee, an Indian term translated to mean either "gathering place by the water" or "beautiful land." You can pretty much take your pick.

The first brewer wasn't German either. A Welshman by the name of Richard Owens produced Milwaukee's first beer, actually ale. But Owens and his Welsh cohorts, William Pawlett and John Davis, were not to have Milwaukee's beer market to themselves for long.

From 1840 to 1860, over 1,350,000 Germans took the long ride from their fatherland to our welcome shores. They came to escape hunger and political and religious oppression, and they came loving picnics and sports and song and hard work ... and beer. "Little Germanys" enlivened many American cities, Milwaukee very definitely included.

Milwaukee, however, had more than just a sizable German community. After his arrival in America in 1854, for example, experienced German brewer Frederick Miller spent a full year traveling throughout much of the United States before selecting Milwaukee as his brewery site ... as much for its fine harbor and plentiful grain and water supplies as for its German populace.

Miller had been preceded by quite a few other German brethren. The first German brewer on the scene, in 1841, was a native of Wurtemberg named Herman Reuthlisberger. Then came August Krug (predecessor of Jos. Schlitz), Frederick Schunck, Jacob Best (predecessor of Pabst), Johann Braun, Stoltz & Krill, etc., etc., etc. Although a few others may be company, a whole host of others is a crowd. Milwaukee was just such a darned good brewing site that there rapidly became too many brewers for even Milwaukee's many thirsty throats. Whereas the brewers of Chicago, New York, Philadelphia, and most of the other huge brewing centers could generally keep profitable and content — as in somewhat fat and lazy — within the confines of their own home

ONE VIEW OF MILWAUKEE. This postcard was mailed back home to Emporia, Kansas, in 1909 ... but the view's not too different today.

38

FRED. MILLER
Brewing Co.

„Miller,
The Best Milwaukee Beer"

Jos. Schlitz
Brewing Co.

„Schlitz,
The Beer
That Made
Milwaukee
Famous"

E. L. Husting,

Ale, Porter,
Weissbeer.

JUNG
BREWING CO.

„Jung Beer
Serves You
Right"

MILWAUKEE
Brewing Co.

BREW
„PRINCE OF PILSEN"

John Graf,

Weissbeer and
Soda Water.

"The Best What
Gives."

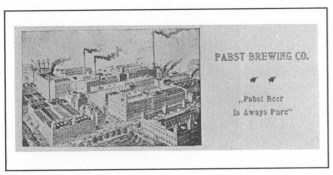

PABST BREWING CO.

„Pabst Beer
Is Aways Pure"

Milwaukee-
Waukesha
Brewing Co.

"The Imperial
Health Beer."

BEER CITY BIGGIES. Some of "The Beer City's" biggies at the turn
of the century. All but Miller and Pabst are gone now, but the fame
they helped to establish lives on.

Continued on next page

PABST IS EVERYWHERE. Pabst probably best exemplified Milwaukee's quest for far-ranging markets. As the pages of this circa 1895 advertising booklet made mighty clear, they considered their market to be … everywhere.

market, the brewers of Milwaukee were forced to look past their not-so-green pastures. They had to hustle, and hustle they did, right from the very beginning. As early as 1856, when the city had twenty-six breweries, more than one-third of their output was already being shipped to other points.

Sad to say, but Chicago's great fire of 1871 allowed Milwaukee beer to get perhaps its greatest leg up. With most of the Windy City's breweries knocked out of commission and its water supply in bad, bad shape, Milwaukee leaped to the rescue, and Chicago found itself awash in Milwaukee beer almost before the fire was out. Some say Chicago's own considerable brewing industry was never the same again. Chicago's beer drinkers had become "Milwaukee-ized." Even that most famed of all beer slogans — Schlitz: The Beer That Made Milwaukee Famous — came out of just this Milwaukee-to-the-rescue effort.

Almost a Century and a Half Later

Today, over 145 years after Milwaukee's first brew kettle was fired up, the city's fame as a brewing center continues. Although Schlitz isn't making Milwaukee famous anymore (it ceased being brewed there in 1981), Miller and Pabst keep Mil-

waukee's tradition alive and well.

And there's a brand-new microbrewery, the Sprecher Brewing Co., started in 1985 by former Pabst employees Randal Sprecher and James Bubolz. Brands are Black Bavarian, Milwaukee Weiss and, pictured here, Sprecher's Special Amber.

Plus Heileman is in the process of building a five million–dollar highly computerized and automated draft-beer-only brewery within the city's limits. And finally, having your city's professional baseball team called the Brewers sure doesn't hurt either!

A HEADSTRONG INFANT. Sprecher's Special Amber, born in 1985 and doing well.

Free Beer on Forty-second Street

The good businessfolk of New York's Forty-second Street like to give you the impression they're giving you a really good deal. "Hey, check it out," they say, almost as if they're giving it away. Well, there was at least one business along Forty-second Street that did give it away. That business was V. Loewer's Gambrinus Brewery, and what they gave away, of course, was beer.

Actually the entrance to Loewer's was on Forty-first Street, 529 West Forty-first, between Tenth and Eleventh Avenues. But the brewery extended through to Forty-second and in fact was one of the more notable structures along the entire length of "the Crossroads of the World."

Loewer's was far from unique in giving away beer. One of the nicer things about many an American brewery — past and present — is that they enjoy giving away free samples. They're proud of their heritage and their product . . . and enjoy sharing it.

As Adolph Geffken, a former New York City beer truck driver, put it:

I liked going to Loewer's. That part of New York was always a calm place. No heavy traffic. We used to drive up, back up to the ramp, and load the truck full of beer.

And the beer was always on tap. You were allowed two glasses of beer, anybody that wanted to walk in. It wasn't just for delivery people; it was for anyone walking down the street. All day long, seven in the morning to four or five in the afternoon. But you'd be surprised . . . very few people would take advantage of it.

V. Loewer's Gambrinus Brewery (1879-1948) . . . where the beer was right out of the tap and the price was right. (Photo courtesy U.S. History, Local History & Genealogy Division, The New York Public Library, Astor, Lenox and Tilden Foundations)

"I don't drink any more than the man next to me, and the man next to me is Dean Martin."

—*Joe E. Lewis*

Who'll Be New York's Favorite Girl?
The Miss Rheingold Contest

A PRETTY GIRL IS LIKE A SWEET SALES MELODY. Philip Liebmann's use of an attractive woman to sell beer was hardly new. Brewers had long known the value of a pretty face. What was new was the involvement of the public in the selection of that pretty face. Colorfully designed ballot boxes were seemingly everywhere, in bars, eateries, grocery stores in and around New York. There were over thirty-five thousand such "polling places" by the mid-1950s. During the August-September voting period all you had to do was decide which contestant you most wanted to look at in newspaper, magazine, subway, and billboard advertising for the next twelve months, check off that name on the ballot, and drop it in the ballot box. You didn't have to buy anything — frozen peas, mushroom gravy, beer, anything — to vote, and you could vote as many times as you wanted. What a sense of power!

I remember running from store to store, grabbing as many ballots as I could. In the neighborhood there sure wasn't talk about the election for mayor or governor . . . but when it came to the Miss Rheingold Contest, everybody was involved. The talk was all about it. Everybody talked about it . . . and everybody voted.
— *John Corrado, resident of East Harlem, New York City during the 1940s and 1950s.*

Yes, everybody certainly voted. And voted. And voted. Ten or fifteen votes cast at a clip was nothing; twenty or thirty votes, now that was a worthwhile effort.

Miss Rheingold Contest-time was the only time of the year I actually hoped my mother would ask (tell!) me to run downtown to Louie's Market to get some frozen peas or a can of mushroom gravy. After all, how exciting are frozen peas? But the duel to be Miss Rheingold . . . now that was exciting! Sometimes it was more than exciting.

If you were pulling for — and voting for — Pat Burrage while Tony Toughissimo was pulling for — and voting for — Liz Hastings, it could be downright dangerous. "Intellectual discussion" as to who should win might all too easily turn into physical confrontation: "Whaddya mean 'Pat Burrage is better looking than Liz Hastings'? Whaddya, blind or somethin'?"

The Miss Rheingold Contest was SERIOUS business.

How it all started was less than serious. It was accidental. The story goes that a printing salesman called upon Liebmann Brewery president Philip Liebmann early in 1940. The salesman's sample kit included several shots of Jinx Falkenburg, at the time a semi-actress, semi-celebrity best known for her tennis playing. Ms. Falkenburg's photos were part of a batch being used to demonstrate a new printing process the salesman's firm had developed.

Recalled Philip Liebmann twenty years later: "The printing process was revolutionary, but the girl was spectacular. I thought she might be what we needed to promote our beer. We decided to put her under contract for 1940 and hitch our publicity to that face. For the next months she appeared in our advertising, and we were very happy with the results. In 1941 we did it a little differently: we let our dealers pick a girl from a folder we sent out bearing pictures of a couple of dozen beauties. In 1942 the voting was left to the public, and from a count of two hundred thousand then, the interest has grown each year. The total votes for Miss Rheingold 1959 exceeded twenty-two million. Only one other election in the country draws more attention at the polls, and I don't need to identify *that* one."

"*That* one," of course, was the presidential election . . . and it wasn't held every year.

Alas, though, the presidential election is still held, still with us, but the Miss Rheingold Contest is long gone. Miss Rheingold of 1964, Celeste Yarnall, was the last winner elected by public vote. The

1965 Miss Rheingold, Sharon Vaughn, was selected by the brewery rather than the public, just as Jinx Falkenburg had been crowned a quarter of a century earlier.

Miss Vaughn was to be the last Miss Rheingold. The official reason given by the brewery for the demise of the contest was waning interest on the part of the public. The unofficial—and probably truer—reason was that Liebmann was rapidly sliding into a no-win situation. If they were to continue to have only lily-white Miss Rheingold contestants, the important black and Hispanic markets would feel cheated; but if a black or Hispanic were to win, the company could genuinely fear white backlash. If there's no way to win, why bother to play? Liebmann decided not to. And so ended one of New York's most famous—and certainly most fun—annual traditions.

Going to the store for frozen peas was never to be the same again.

SHE STARTED IT ALL. If Jinx Falkenburg, who was featured in several mostly forgettable movies and was a radio personality in both the "Hi, Jinx" and "Tex & Jinx" radio shows, hadn't been so good looking, there probably would never have been a Miss Rheingold Contest. Here she is looking mighty appealing in a pair of posed studio shots. Philip Liebmann had good taste!

Several examples of pre-Prohibition "girlie" beer advertising, including a 1905 calendar from Liebmann's itself that showed considerably more than just a pretty face.

Continued on next page

JANET MICK
Miss Rheingold 1961

"SORT OF A LARK." To enter the Miss Rheingold Contest you had to be a registered model and show up for the preliminary judging, held in New York City at the Waldorf-Astoria. As many as two thousand hopefuls did, many more for the fun of it than with any serious view of winning.

This friend of mine said, "You know, why don't you enter the Rheingold contest? It's starting." I entered in the New York competition. I found out where it was and I went up. It was just sort of a lark because they said, "You should go; you should go." So in order to console my friends, I said, "Alright, I'm going."
— *Janet Mick, Miss Rheingold, 1961*

Diane Baker moved quickly from Miss Rheingold contestland and to movieland. She made her film debut in *The Diary of Anne Frank* (1959), followed by *Journey to the Center of The Earth* (1959), *Nine Hours to Rama* (1963), *The Prize* (1963), *Stolen Hours* (1963), *Straightjacket* (1963), *Curse of the Fly* (1965), etc. TV movie credits include *The Old Man Who Cried Wolf* (1971), *A Tree Grows in Brooklyn* (1974), and *The Summer of '69* (1977).

Here she is as she appeared on her very own Rheingold Extra Dry can during the 1957 campaign.

Apart from Jinx Falkenburg, who doesn't really count because she was somewhat of a celebrity before her Miss R. stint and because she received only a fraction of the hoopla of the later, elected Favorite Girls, no Miss Rheingold went on to any great further fame. But three losing contestants did: Tippi Hedren, who lost in the 1953 contest; Hope Lange, who lost in the 1954 contest; and Diane Baker, who lost in the 1957 contest.

PRETTY PLUMS. The 1957 contestants were further immortalized by being pictured on Rheingold's cans. The beer-buying public, however, was less than fully impressed. Very, very few of the cans appear to have been kept and today are exceedingly scarce, a pretty plum on any beer can collector's shelf. And at one thousand dollars or so apiece, they're an expensive pretty plum!

PAT BURRAGE: MISS RHEINGOLD, 1950. Pat Burrage was pretty; heck, she was beautiful. *All* Miss Rheingolds were beautiful: Rita Daigle, Michaele Fallon, Pat Quinlan, Pat McElroy, Pat Burrage, Elise Gammon, Anne Hogan, Mary Austin, Adrienne Garrett, Nancy Woodruff, Hillie Merritt, Margie McNally, Madelyn Darrow, Robbin Bain, Emily Banks, Janet Mick, Kathy Kersh … their names still roll off the tongue easier than a cold Rheingold … especially if their name were Pat: all told, there were four Miss Rheingolds named Pat, including three in a row in 1948, 1949, and, of course, Pat Burrage in 1950.

It Paid to Lose

To the winner of the Miss Rheingold Contest went considerable fame and fortune … up to fifty thousand dollars cash, plus an extensive wardrobe and lots of travel. But the winner was actually less of a winner than might have appeared to be the case, for she became forever after typecast. As Janet Mick, Miss Rheingold of 1961, explains it:

> I was basically interested in continuing into acting. I was studying acting at the time. But when I went out to get work [after being Miss Rheingold] no one wanted to hire me because I was so well associated with Rheingold. I mean, for instance, if I went up to interview for a coffee commercial, they wouldn't use me because people would instantly say, "That's Rheingold, that's Miss Rheingold." So they wouldn't think of a coffee, they'd think of the beer instead.

So in some ways it actually paid to lose. That way you got all the election publicity, but you didn't become typecast as a person whose favorite pronouncement was "My beer is Rheingold, the Dry Beer!"

The Mystery of Arlene Dahlman

Was Arlene Dahl really Arlene Dahlman, or was Arlene Dahlman really Arlene Dahl? One of the losing contestants in the 1949 Miss Rheingold Contest was named Arlene Dahlman. Did she, as Arlene Dahl, go on to considerable success in films such as *Three Little Words* (1950), *Woman's World* (1954), *Wicked As They Come* (1956), etc.? If so, then she joins our list of ex–Miss Rheingold contestants who went on to fame after failing to be more than a contestant.

45

Those Other "Misses"

STANDING TALL. Seven of the contestants vying for the honor of being Miss Tavern Pale strutted their stuff for the camera in this spring 1949 publicity shot.

An opinionated opinion: about five of 'em should've stayed home.

JACOB SCHMIDT'S CHOICE. Gretchen Palen, Miss City Club of 1951, shows off her smile and her five thousand–dollar mink coat.

Said the brewery of Miss Palen: "Gretchen Palen is our choice, and a happy choice, for Miss City Club of 1951. She's a girl of many talents: model . . . dancer . . . skater."

Said the brewery of City Club Beer: "Make City Club your happy choice: it's mellow dry, with just enough tang to make every drink sparkle from sip to swallow."

Today both City Club and Miss City Club are just distant memories in Twin Cityland. Jacob Schmidt is still very much in business, a division of Heileman, but they dropped City Club from their product line in 1959.

If, as the saying goes, imitation is the sincerest form of flattery, then there was a whole mess of flattering going on in the 1940s and 1950s. Inspired by the success of Miss Rheingold, a host of brewers from coast to coast inaugurated their own "Miss" spectacle.

At various and diverse times during the forties and fifties there was a Miss Tavern Pale . . . Tavern Pale Beer, Atlantic Brewing Co., Chicago; Miss City Club . . . City Club Beer, Jacob Schmidt Brewing Co., St. Paul; Miss Red Top . . . Red Top Beer & Ale, Red Top Brewing Co., Cincinnati; Miss Maryland TV . . . American Brewing Co., Baltimore.

Then there were double "Misses." The Fox Head Brewing Co. of Waukesha, Wisconsin, had a Miss Fox Head 400 Light Beer and a Miss Fox Head 400 Dark Beer. The Galveston-Houston Breweries of Galveston, Texas, used full-page ads to promote its contest for the Southern Select Twins in 1954. If you were down Texas-way that year you could vote between four sets of twins. Heralded the brewery's ads: "Choose the beautiful twin girls you want to see represent the beer that's <u>Double Good</u> . . . Southern Select."

And there was a triple "Miss." Philadelphia's Jacob Hornung Brewing Co. held a series of three-month–long contests leading to the crowning of a Miss Hornung Beer, a Miss Londonderry Ale, and last but not at all least, a Miss Hornung Bock Beer.

Even Heineken got in the act in 1951. They had a Dutch Miss . . . the most beautiful Dutch girl in America. Selected out of over one thousand applicants was a woman with the good Dutch-sounding name of Cathy Van Hild.

And lastly there were a couple of "Misses" who weren't "Misses." The Gunther Brewing Co. of Baltimore touted its Gunther Girl, Rosemary Colligan, while further west the Goebel Brewing Co. of Detroit and Muskegon, Michigan, and Oakland, California, sang the merits of its beauty, Evelyn Johnson, the Goebel Girl.

Only a few of these "Other Miss" promos went the full Miss Rheingold route, crowning their "Miss" by public vote. The selection of Miss Maryland TV, Phyllis Maygers, in 1951 was a notable exception. Well over one million votes were cast, the most ever for any election held in Baltimore up to that time.

But whether elected or selected, the many brewery "Misses" of the 1940s and 1950s can all trace their lineage back to 1940, the year Jinx Falkenburg popped out of a batch of salesmen's samples and infatuated Philip Liebmann.

"Good Ale, Raw Onions, and No Ladies"

"Good ale, raw onions, and no ladies" ... such was the motto at John McSorley's famed New York pub on East Seventh Street for 116 years.

John McSorley (1823–1910) was a good Irishman (are there any other kind?!) who came to New York City via his native County Tyrone and founded in 1854 a drinking establishment he originally called the Old House at Home.

So it was named until 1908, when a strong wind blew the Old House sign down. John took this as an omen that a name change was called for and he came up with the handle McSorley's Old Ale House. Thus it has been ever since.

But back to John's motto. His feeling about ale, onions, and the ladies was more than a mere saying. It was a rule. Except for a very short experiment with booze, the hard stuff, back in 1905, only good ale —light and dark— has been served at McSorley's since John, himself, drew the first mug, probably for himself, lo those many years ago.

Onions—the fresh, raw variety—are still a specialty of the house at McSorley's, no meal quite complete without them. John, when he was master of the kitchen as well as the bar, liked nothing better than to wedge a whole raw onion into the middle of a loaf of French bread and savor the combination as if it were an apple.

And the ladies ... well they were just plain not welcome. John had a conviction —and a strong one at that—that it was impossible for men to enjoy their drinking if women were around. So he made sure they weren't. If a damsel chanced to venture in, he'd just escort her right back out. "Madam, I'm sorry, but we don't serve ladies," he'd say. And that's the way it remained until 1970, when under threat of legal action McSorley's finally relented and allowed women in. There's still but one bathroom, however, and in an establishment that serves only ale, that can—and does —lead to some rather interesting situational dialogues.

Today McSorley's is pretty much yuppie city. Would John McSorley have minded? Probably not in the least. Ah, but the ladies ... he'd mind about that. He'd be mighty upset that women were cluttering up his domain, his place of drinking and fellowship, his place of "good ale, raw onions ... and no ladies."

AT McSORLEY'S ONE HUN-DREDTH BIRTHDAY PARTY. When New York's oldest operating bar hit the ripe old age of one hundred on February 18, 1954, the boys were busy having a jolly good time celebrating both inside and outside ... (Photo courtesy *New York News*)

... while Dorothy Kirwan, McSorley's owner, contented herself celebrating from the sidewalk only. Sure, she could have gone in. After all, it was her place. But Ms. Kirwan felt strongly that John McSorley's wishes should be honored, so she did her toasting from the outside looking in. (Photo courtesy *New York News*)

"The Hamm's Man of the Midwest" ... and His Favorite Bear

The Hamm's Bear, introduced as the symbol for Hamm's Beer in 1954, has amused, beguiled, and captivated beer drinkers and non-beer drinkers alike for over thirty years. To get the lowdown on the bear — and his personal fascination with it — *From Beer to Eternity* asked Jim Welytok of Milwaukee to tell us all about it. Here's what "The Hamm's Man of the Midwest" had to say:

I guess I've been collecting for a little over eight years now. For me it all started with a single Hamm's sign. I was babysitting for my niece at the time, and while trying to keep her amused, I started digging through my brother-in-law's closet looking for games. Instead I came across a Hamm's beer sign.

Well, I plugged it in and ended up amusing myself. I told my brother-in-law I had to have that sign, and I finally did receive it for my birthday some six months later, but by then I had already been out buying all types of beer advertising at garage sales, flea markets, auctions, etc.

They Thought I'd Gone Nuts

My whole family thought I had gone nuts, coming home every weekend with all this, as they called it, "junk." I didn't let them discourage me, though. I really enjoyed all the neat stuff I bought. Especially the Hamm's signs. I took an exceptional interest in Hamm's items right from the start. Hamm's put an extremely high dollar amount into their point of purchase advertising. Their

YEP, JIM'S IN THERE SOMEWHERE. Jim and a small part of his Hamm's collection. Jim himself is a little tough to spot in the photo ... but he's there, proudly amidst all the bears and other Hamm's breweriana.

advertising items were more than just signs, they got the consumer's attention. Their theme was very appealing, with the background of deep north woods and the land of sky blue waters. Just mention Hamm's beer signs to anyone, whether they collect beer signs or not, and there are two or more things that people always remember — the classic Hamm's moving water sign, which I've heard numerous stories about, and of course the famous Hamm's Bear, which most everyone is familiar with through his outrageous situations in television commercials. The Hamm's Bear has always appealed to me; I guess that's why I started to specialize in bear items about seven years ago.

Known as "The Hamm's Man of the Midwest"

It has taken a long time for me to be known as "The Hamm's Man of the Midwest," but it's slowly working out. Most of my better advertising pieces come to me from other collectors who know I'm serious about Hamm's items. However, because of all the competition, it's gotten to the point where it's really hard to find a nice piece on my own. At every flea market or auction I go to, I always run into a herd of fellow collectors; and while it's nice to socialize, it doesn't always make for a very good buying atmosphere. So when I do find a nice item on my own, it's really satisfying and reason to celebrate.

One of my best finds happened after I received a tip from someone at a flea market. I was selling signs at my booth at the time when a lady came along saying that her father had designed Hamm's signs for over thirty years. I could hardly believe it! He was deceased, but she was sure there were still some things in his basement studio. Well, as it turned out, there was. I picked up blueprints on how the bear and friends must be drawn, several pencil sketches, animated signs, and even some plans for signs that, to the best of my knowledge, were never produced.

She Knew I'd Really Appreciate It

Best of all, I received all these priceless articles for free! His widow was happy to give it all to someone who would really appreciate it. Believe me, I do!

Another Really Good Find

Another really good find was the time a guy called me up saying he had some Hamm's stuff from when he worked at the brewery. Without delay we met and I wound up with some genuine Cleo Hovel artwork, over two hours of Hamm's TV commercials, and a lot of Hamm's information on paper, again all for free. He said it didn't cost him anything, so he didn't feel right selling it. He had heard about me and my collection and felt it would be well preserved among my other Hamm's artifacts. He was right; It will be well preserved and very much appreciated. To me finds like these are overwhelming, too few and far between.

One of the Most Rewarding Things

But one of the most rewarding things about my collecting experiences, which was not foreseen nor realized until a few years ago, is all the long-lasting, good friendships that have been formed with fellow collectors across the country.

About America's Favorite Bear (Well, Beer Bear Anyway)

From his home in St. Paul (where Theodore Hamm first started brewing his beer in 1865), the Hamm's Bear lumbered his way into the hearts and funnybones of much of America. In 1965, at one of the peaks of his popularity, research conducted by the Audit Research Bureau, for instance, showed that the bear consistently ranked number one in terms of best-liked ads. What's more amazing is that the bureau's research measured people's views on a national scale . . . but Hamm's commercials were only aired in thirty-one states. The bear's popularity was of such a magnitude that it overcame the nineteen-state disadvantage.

A NICE GUY FROM MILWAUKEE. Jim Welytok, a big-league collector of Hamm's Bear breweriana if ever there was one. What's a nice guy from Milwaukee doing saving stuff from a St. Paul, Minnesota, brewery?! "The Hamm's Bear has always appealed to me" is Jim's very ready — and very appropriate — answer.

THE Just Having Fun Drinking BEER in the Neighborhood Bar GAME

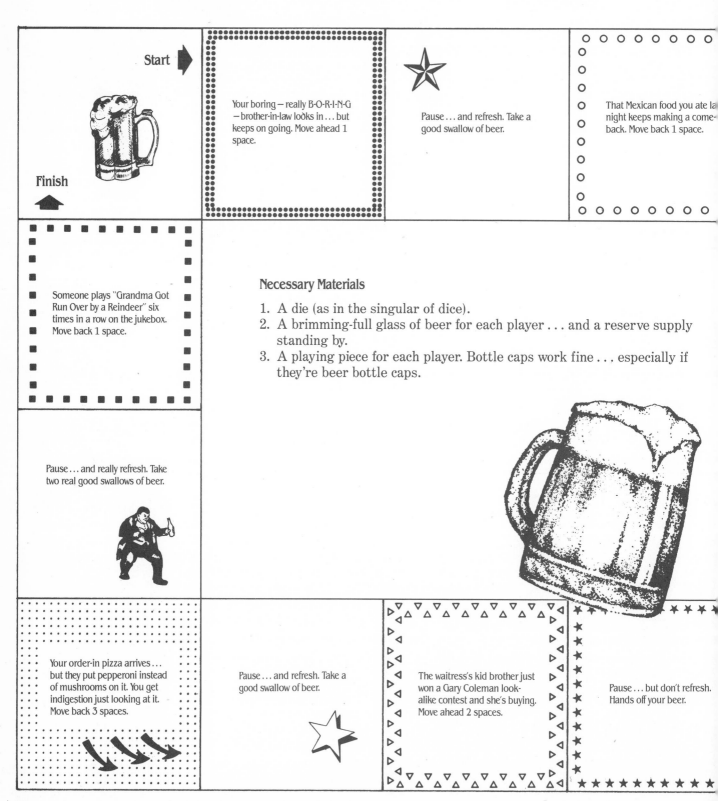

Start ➤

Finish

Your boring — really B-O-R-I-N-G — brother-in-law looks in... but keeps on going. Move ahead 1 space.

Pause... and refresh. Take a good swallow of beer.

That Mexican food you ate last night keeps making a comeback. Move back 1 space.

Someone plays "Grandma Got Run Over by a Reindeer" six times in a row on the jukebox. Move back 1 space.

Necessary Materials

1. A die (as in the singular of dice).
2. A brimming-full glass of beer for each player... and a reserve supply standing by.
3. A playing piece for each player. Bottle caps work fine... especially if they're beer bottle caps.

Pause... and really refresh. Take two real good swallows of beer.

Your order-in pizza arrives... but they put pepperoni instead of mushrooms on it. You get indigestion just looking at it. Move back 3 spaces.

Pause... and refresh. Take a good swallow of beer.

The waitress's kid brother just won a Gary Coleman look-alike contest and she's buying. Move ahead 2 spaces.

Pause... but don't refresh. Hands off your beer.

Pause ... but don't refresh.
Hands off your beer.

A garbage truck crashes through the front door, but the only damage done is to the garbage. The driver buys beer all around. Move ahead 3 spaces.

Refresh ... but don't pause. Take a good swallow of beer and roll again.

You hear on the news that the hot stock you just bought dropped 26 points today. Move back 3 spaces.

Rules of Play

1. Any number of people — from 2 to 102 — may play.
2. The thirstiest player moves first, the second thirstiest moves second, etc.
3. Each player keeps on rolling and moving until he or she lands on a space that says "Pause." He or she pauses and the next player rolls.
4. The first player to cross the finish line is THE WINNER, and all other players must buy the winner a beer. The second player to cross the finish line is THE SECOND-PLACE WINNER, and all remaining players must buy the second-place winner a beer. This continues down to THE LAST-PLACE WINNER, who buys himself/herself a beer.

Everyone's a winner in THE Just Having Fun Drinking BEER in the Neighborhood Bar GAME!

Pause ... but don't refresh.
Hands off your beer.

The bartender's wife just had a baby, and he's sporting a smile as big as a brewhouse. Move ahead 3 spaces.

The 280-pound woman sitting next to you spills her diet cola all over you. Move back 3 spaces.

Pause ... and refresh. Take a good swallow of beer.

There are new "poetic thoughts" on the rest room wall ... and they've got you really chuckling. Move ahead 1 space.

Refresh ... but don't pause. Take a good swallow of beer and roll again.

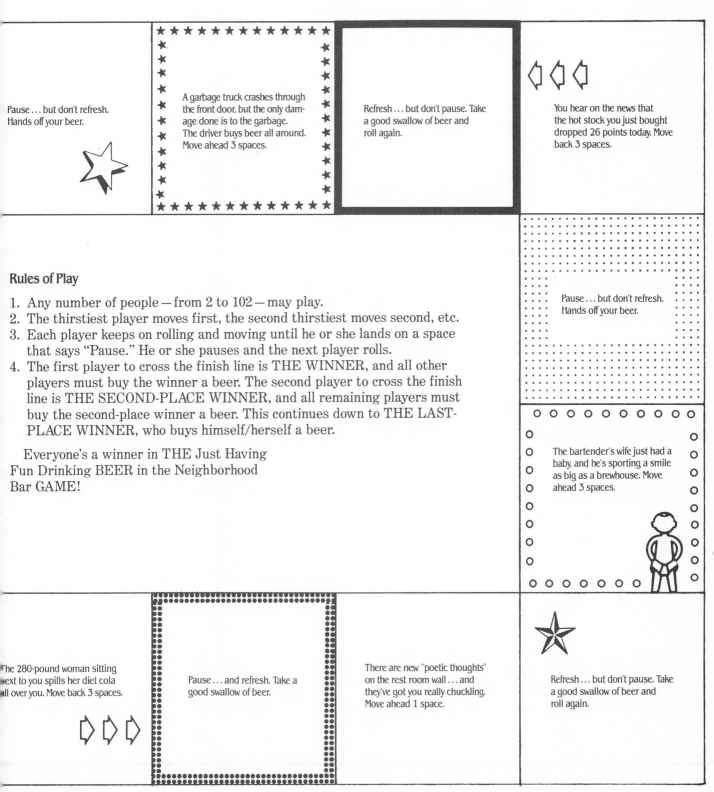

When Guinness Stout Was Brewed in the U.S.A.

Circa 1950 tap knob

BURKE'S SUPERIOR ALE. It may have been superior, but it wasn't successful.

Who is there this side of Killarney that does not know the "Guinness Stout... Ah, Sweet Guinness Stout" song?

> Guinness Stout... ah, sweet
> Guinness Stout
> Just one or two delicious sips
> Passing through my thirsty lips
> And it's St. Pat's Day
> With sweet Rosie O'Grady going
>   my way...
> On the storied streets of Dublin.

Very good. But bet a pint you don't know the second verse.

> Guinness Stout... ah, sweet
>   Guinness Stout
> Just one or two delicious sips
> Passing through my thirsty lips
> And it's St. Pat's Day
> With sweet Rosie O'Grady going my
>   way...
> On the storied streets of Long Island
>   City.

Yep, Long Island City. For fifteen years, from 1939 to 1954, Guinness's Stout was brewed right here in the U.S.A. In Long Island City, New York.

The story starts in 1933. An English firm by the name of E. & J. Burke decided the time was right to build a brewery in the New World. Burke had its fingers in a number of pies. In England it bottled Guinness's Stout for export. In America it was the sole agent for Perrier water, was the sole importer — and had been for almost a century — of Bass Ale and Guinness's Stout, and distributed a line of soft drinks under the C & C name.

Now it would do its own brewing, too. A brand new brew complex was constructed on a site bounded by Forty-seventh Avenue, Twenty-seventh and Twenty-eighth Streets, and Skillman Avenue in Long Island City, just an empty half-barrel's throw from Manhattan.

Burke's Ale, Burke's Beer, and Burke's Stout were all soon bubbling out of the new facility, only to be greeted with but modest success. Just another small brewery doing its thing. The winds of war, however, gave Burke its real shot at success. Concerned that the fast-approaching conflict with Germany would cut America's Guinness supply lines, the powers that be in Dublin gave the green light in 1939 to begin brewing the reknowned stout here. And so it was–under both the E. & J. Burke and Arthur Guinness Son & Co. names — until 1954.

It should have succeeded... but it didn't. The problem was basic, very basic: when a person's thirst turned to a Guinness, he or she wanted that thirst satisfied with "the real thing" — stout brewed in Ireland. In Dublin. Long Island City? Forget it! It didn't even sound Irish!

Long Island City-brewed Guinness's Stout... less than a mashing success. For too many people, if it wasn't brewed in the old sod, it just wasn't kosher.

Guinness also tried licensing its name to the Goebel Brewing Co., of Detroit and Muskegon, Michigan, and Oakland, California, for Guinness's Beer and Guinness's Ale. Brewed from 1949 through 1955, it met with little more success than did its Long Island City cousin.

52

A Brewer, a Baker, a Candlestick Maker

Guinness and "Good for You" have sounded well together almost since the famed brewery's beginnings in 1759, the year Arthur Guinness founded his brewery in the St. James gate section of Dublin. Harry Grattan, one of Ireland's foremost members of Parliament, once declared Guinness to be the "nurse of the people."

E. & J. BURKE. They'd have been better off just sticking wih Perrier!

1937 *Fortune* ad

Vassar College was founded by

   (a) a brewer
   (b) a baker
   (c) a candlestick maker

MATTHEW VASSAR. Not a baker, not a candlestick maker . . . and not a brewer of lager either.

If your answer is a baker or a candlestick maker, it is hereby suggested that you dine, not *by* candlesticks, but *on* candlesticks for the next fortnight!

Vassar College was founded by a brewer!

It was America's first privately endowed college for women and was founded by Poughkeepsie, New York, ale brewer Matthew Vassar. Matthew's father, James, started brewing in Poughkeepsie in the late 1790s. From 1810 on, Matthew was a partner in the firm, although he began to lose interest in brewing in the 1850s as he pursued his idea of an institution of higher learning for women. In 1861 his dream came true: Vassar Female College was chartered. Six years later, in 1867, the name was changed to its present-day Vassar College.

Although the college Matthew Vassar endowed has fared well through the years, his brewery did not. Vassar stubbornly stuck to brewing only beer in the British tradition . . . ale, porter, and stout. He refused to switch any of his output to the ever-more popular lager. It was a stubbornness that proved disastrous, and the once prosperous Vassar Brewery closed its doors in 1896, twenty-eight years after Matthew Vassar's death in 1868. He still lives on, however, in Vassar legend and song:

> And so you see, for old V.C.
> Our love shall never fail.
> Full well we know
> That we owe
> To Matthew Vassar's ale!

53

Bock Beer: It Used to Be a Big Deal

When was the last time you had a glass of bock beer? Have you ever had a glass of bock beer?

If you're under forty or forty-five, the chances are that you've never had a glass of bock beer because the beverage that was once brewing's sweet harbinger of spring has been pretty much relegated to oblivion, lost in the crush toward ever lighter and lighter beers. More's the pity, too, for bock's taste is as intriguing as the legends that surround it.

What Is Bock Beer?

First, what bock beer is not: it is *not* the dregs cleaned out of brewing vats in the spring. How the dregs rumor got started is anybody's guess, but it's a rumor with absolutely no basis in fact.

The distinctive flavor and dark brown hue of the special brew is the result of the roasted or caramelized malt that is used in brewing it. It is also often aged longer than lighter beers. It has traditionally made its appearance in the spring.

Historians believe bock had its origins in the fourth or fifth centuries among the tribes of northern Europe. As part of the annual harvesting of crops, the very best grains were selected, steeped in water chosen by the tribe's priests, brewed into beer, and then placed in underground caves to age all through the winter. With the arrival of spring, the beer was brought forth, consumed with great relish and ceremony, and blessings were offered both as thanks for the previous fall's harvest and in the hope of a bounteous crop in the year ahead.

Although the significance of bock changed down through the centuries, its symbol as a sign of spring did not. Until relatively recently a placard with a goat on it displayed in a tavern window was as sure a way of knowing it was spring as was seeing a robin or having the urge to get out the old baseball glove.

Why a Goat?

Why a goat instead of an elephant or an anteater or a pigeon? And while we're at it, whence cometh the word *bock*?

Basically historians are uncertain with respect to both of these questions, but they've had fun trying to figure them out! One theory holds that two rival German brewers happened to meet in a tavern way back when. Each was outspoken on the merits of his own brew ... and the demerits of his rival's. After much jawing, they decided to settle things once and for all. Each brewer was to wolf down (goat down?) as much of his rival's beer as he could. The winner would be the one who could stand on his feet and keep drinking the longest ... as that would prove his beer was the strongest. After many hours, and as things were winding down and both contestants fading fast, one of the two ventured to the door for some air. Just then a goat sauntered in, banged into the quite tipsy brewer, and knocked him off his feet. "I win!" declared the still-standing brewer. "It was the goat," snarled the loser from his perch on the floor. What he actually snarled was "It was the bock," because bock is the German word for goat. Word of the contest spread,

Bock beer cans from the 1930s, 1940s, and 1950s are even rarer than bock itself today. Cans of this vintage—in pristine condition—regularly sell among beer can collectors (serious beer can collectors, obviously!) for one thousand dollars ... and up.

and bock came to be the accepted name for stronger, heartier brew.

A second, entirely different story revolves around the city of Einbeck, Germany. During the Middle Ages, Einbeck was famed throughout Europe for its superior quality beer, especially its dark beer. The city's name was sometimes spelled *Eimbock* and often pronounced that way regardless of its spelling. It's thus theorized that people requesting Einbeck beer would call out "Ein Bock" and that eventually this became shortened to just plain "bock."

Then there are those who feel that the word *bock* most likely comes from astrology. After all, goes this theory, the special brew was made from grains brewed under the sign of Capricorn, the goat. Goat is *bock* in German, etc., etc.

Three different theories. Each somewhat plausible; each somewhat implausible. Take your pick. But more important, why not seek out bock the next time spring rolls around? It's difficult to find but well worth giving it a try. Some people characterize the brew's taste as murky or musty; others as dark or even dangerous. Whatever, you'll know you're drinking something different!

OH! JOY! This is how the Hubert Fischer Brewery of Hartford, Connecticut, heralded the arrival of its bock in 1913. Joy, oh joy! Boy, oh boy!

MR. EINBOCK, I PRESUME. In days of old, a goat sign in the window of Ye Olde Neighborhood Tavern could only mean two things...bock beer was here and so was spring.

Continued on next page

Oh, You Handsome Goat!

One of the highlights of the bock beer season in New York City in the mid-1930s was the Mr. Bock Beer Contest. Owners of male goats with "large horns and gentle dispositions" were encouraged to enter their goats in the contest. The final judging was held in Central Park by the same panel that judged the Miss America Pageant in Atlantic City.

This is "Pretzels," Mr. Bock Beer for 1934.

In addition to the selection of Mr. Bock, the Big Apple—and many other cities across the nation— had an annual Bock Beer Festival complete with bockburgers, bockwurst, bockdogs, and, of course, barrels and barrels of bock beer.

Circa 1952 R & H coaster

"THE BREWERY NEEDS THE EMPTIES." Blimp or no blimp, R & H had less than a peerless reputation among the majority of New York's beer drinkers. There were even those quaffers given to saying that R & H stood for *Rotten & Horrible.* Sales slid, and by 1953, the brewery had plenty of empties. In fact, all empties: Rubsam & Horrmann was sold to Piel's, and the R & H brand name was discontinued.

The R & H Blimp

I s it a bird? Is it a plane? No, it's the R & H blimp.

Or, rather, it *was* the R & H blimp. Neither R & H nor its blimp is doing much flying nowadays, but in the late 1940s both were right up there. R & H (short for Rubsam & Horrmann, the brewery's full name) was Staten Island's sole brewery, and its R & H Beer was a steady seller in and around New York City. In an attempt to increase those sales, the brewery dreamed up its blimp extravaganza in 1947.

The blimp did, indeed, create quite a sight in the two-plus years it floated over New York and surrounding states. The unavailability of helium caused it to be grounded in 1949.

R & H'ing it above the Big Apple, circa 1948

LONGER THAN A CITY BLOCK. Imagine a spectacularly lighted beer ad longer than a city block and six stories high floating above you in the darkness of night, and you begin to imagine the impact of the R & H blimp. By day, painted letters forty-two feet high proclaimed "R & H Beer." At night, the

letters were but twenty-seven feet high but more dramatic. A running sign composed of more than ten thousand light bulbs flashed out different R & H slogans. The outline of the blimp wasn't visible; therefore, the slogans seemed to be floating in midair. Talk about—pardon the pun—high drama!

Did You Hear What One Cockroach Said to the Other?

Let me ask you a personal question: *Do you have a cockroach problem?*

That's pretty personal.

Well not to worry, beer comes through again. Seems there aren't too many things cockroaches love more than beer. Shows they have good taste, doesn't it? But it's a taste that goes overboard, that turns them into veritable beer lushes. And apparently the bigger the cockroach, the bigger the beer lush.

Now down in Texas—of course—they have the biggest cockroaches you can find anywhere. There are tales around Houston of the critters growing up to be three inches long . . . almost the size of a teenage armadillo. To grow that big, Texas roaches aren't awfully bashful about what they eat: chili, corn pone, lots of barbeque, steak . . . even quiche. But to wash it down, like any good Texan, they want a Lone Star or a Shiner or a Pearl. And the more they have, the more they want, which is their downfall.

To get 'em, an old Texas trick is to fill up a big bowl with beer and leave it out at bedtime. The roaches, out for their night on your town, will almost immediately pick up the fragrant aroma of malt and hops on their antennae, dive in, and begin to drink. And drink. And drink. Except for the one or two teetotalers in the crowd, the critters'll drink so much they'll lose control, pass out, and drown.

Gooey, gooey. But effective. And as one cockroach said to the other: "What a way to go!"

Bloomie's Best

Bloomingdale's has been a fixture on New York's East Side for so many years now that some people probably think it's been there forever . . . almost forever, anyway. There was life at Fifty-ninth Street and Third Avenue before Bloomie's, however, and it involved none other than malt and hops . . . and Henry Elias and George Schmitt. Mssrs. Elias and Schmitt operated a brewery on Bloomingdale's present site from 1865 to 1868. It was a modest operation, described as "an antiquated affair," with a "diminutive mash tub" and other primitive equipment "laid down upon a rickety floor," but it was a brewery nonetheless. And were the brewery to have somehow strangely survived all these years, Bloomie's would undoubtedly be merchandising it as Bloomingdale's Beer Boutique . . . with Bloomie's Best selling for something like sixteen dollars a six-pack.

George Schmitt, Sr.

Henry Elias.

Bloomie's as it appeared a hundred years ago.

Who's King of the Hill?

The "King of Beers" is Budweiser. Even your average kindergartner knows that. But what your average kindergartner doesn't know is that Budweiser wasn't always king of the hill. Other "kings" roared, too.

Close to home, right in Budweiser's own St. Louis stomping grounds, the American Brewing Co. billed its St. Louis A. B. C. Bohemian, in pre-Prohibition days, as "King of All Bottled Beers." Even closer yet, right within Anheuser-Busch, Michelob was touted as "King of Draught Beer." And at least two brewers used the identical "King of Beers" slogan. Detroit's Regal Brewing Co. claimed their Regal Beer to be "King of Beers," while New York City's Beadleston & Woerz did likewise for its Imperial Beer.

But that was some time ago. Monarchs fall, kings are dethroned. Sitting up there all alone now there's just one "King of Beers" . . . Budweiser.

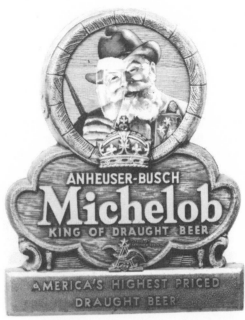

"AMERICA'S HIGHEST PRICED DRAUGHT BEER." A 1930s sign-selling Michelob as not only "King of Draught Beer" but as "America's Highest Priced Draught Beer," too. Michelob has been an important part of the Anheuser-Busch family since it was introduced in 1896.

PURITY, EXCELLENCE, WORLD-RENOWNED. Turn-of-the-century sales piece for St. Louis A. B. C. Bohemian Beer. As with Beadleston & Woerz, the American Brewing Co. was not modest in its claims!

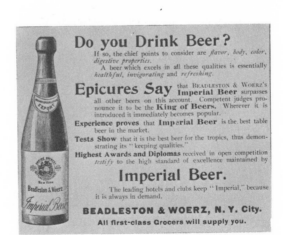

THE KING OF THE HILL. Budweiser . . . the King that still rules.

"DO YOU DRINK BEER?" "King of Beers" is just one of the many claims made by Beadleston & Woerz for its Imperial Beer in this circa 1895 ad. Beadleston & Woerz, located on West Tenth Street near the Hudson River, went out of business with the onset of Prohibition in 1920. Its Imperial Beer — "King of Beers" and all — went with it.

59

The All-time Beer Name Baseball Team

There are *all* kinds of all-time baseball teams: All-time Cleveland Indians Team; All-time Black Team; All-time Polish Team; All-time Free Agent Team; All-time West Virginia Panhandle Team; etc., etc. But it's time for all those other all-time teams to step aside, way aside. Now taking the field for the first time anytime anywhere is the All-time Beer Name Baseball Team. George Steinbrenner, eat your heart out.

Leading off and playing first base is BUD Hassett, a seven-year veteran of the (Brooklyn) Dodgers, (Boston) Braves, and Yankees in the late thirties and early forties. Has a lifetime batting average of .292 and batted over .290 in five of his seven seasons.

Batting second and playing right field is Dick PORTER, an unsung .308 lifetime hitter for the Indians and Red Sox in the 1930s. Batted .350 in 1930, his first full season in the bigs.

In the third slot and doing the catching is none other than Lawrence "Yogi" BEERA (that's right, BEERA: if Lawrence can become Yogi, why can't Berra become Beera?!). One of the finest clutch hitters in the game's history, Yogi hit 358 home runs and drove in 1,430 runners in his eighteen years with the Yankees. He was elected to the Baseball Hall of Fame in 1971.

Hitting cleanup and holding down the hot corner is the Pride of the Phillies, Mike SCHMIDT. With 495 lifetime homers through 1986, the redhead from Dayton has led the National League in that category eight times. This shoo-in future Hall of Famer is no slouch with the glove either.

Batting fifth and very ably patrolling center field is Bing MILLER, a .312 lifetime hitter over a most distinguished sixteen-year span with the Senators, Browns, Red Sox, and (Philadelphia) Athletics. Best known as a standout on Connie Mack's Philadelphia powerhouse pennant winners of 1929–1931.

In the sixth slot and playing left field is Johnny HOP (yep, I'm cheating a little again, but I once saw Roy Campanella on an All-time Italian Team: that's really cheating!). "Hippity" Hop played on five pennant winners in the forties and early fifties, batting .336 for the Cards in 1944 and .333 for the (Boston) Braves in 1946. Had a career average of .296.

Hitting seventh and playing a dandy second base is Germany SCHAEFER. Germany (real name Harold: I'd have changed it, too) played for a host of teams in the early years of the century and sported a lifetime average of .257 over his fifteen years in the majors.

In the eighth slot and playing a heck of a shortshop is BUD Harrelson. The spark plug of the Mets' 1969 and 1973 National League championships, Bud played an even 1,400 games at shortstop in his sixteen years with the Mets and Phillies.

All the way from Meridian, Mississippi, comes our starting pitcher, Dennis "OIL CAN" Boyd. Around Meridian, beer is often referred

Awesome as it is, the All-time Beer Name Baseball Team has been put together using only American beer names of today. Think how doubly (triply?) awesome we could be if we got into imports (George FOSTER and his fifty-two home runs in 1977 comes readily to mind) or oldies but goodies (for starters there used to be beers called WAGNER and JOHNSON . . . as in Honus and Walter).

DUGOUT

The team's in the dugout now, but when they take the field . . . watch out!

LF
Johnny HOPP
1939–1952

CF
Bing
MILLER
1921–1936

RF
Dick
PORTER
1929–1934

2B
Germany
SCHAEFER
1901–1918

SS
BUD
Harrelson
1965–1980

1B
BUD
Hassett
1936–1942

P
OIL CAN
Boyd
1982–

3B
Mike
SCHMIDT
1972–

C

E
Yogi BERRA
1946–1965

60

to as "oil." Legend has it that Dennis's fondness for beer — whence came the Oil Can nickname — was exceeded only by his fondness for baseball. The hard-throwing righty has won forty-three games for Boston over the last three seasons, appears to be a real comer.

Other starters include Tom BREWER, who won ninety-one games for the Red Sox from 1954–1961 (including a 19–9 year in 1956); Allyn "Fish Hook" STOUT, who toiled in an undistinguished fashion for a trio of National League teams from 1931 to 1935 and then bounced back to win one more game for the (Boston) Braves in 1943; and Clarence BEERS, who had a 13.50 ERA in a total of one game for the Cards in 1948 (but with a name as good as Beers — plural no less — we can certainly overlook his otherwise unimpressive credentials!).

Should the unlikely occur and "OIL CAN," Tom, "Fish Hook," or Clarence need relief, we have it with a capital Stu and a capital Jim. Stu MILLER was a reliever par excellence for numerous teams in a sixteen-year career that stretched from 1952 to 1968. Best years were 14–5 for the Giants in 1961 and 14–7 for the Orioles in 1965, all in relief. Add Jim BREWER and his seventeen years of relief work — and career 3.07 ERA — for the Cubs, Dodgers, and Angels from 1960 through 1976, and we come up with a pitching staff to make any beer drinker's mouth water.

The All-time Beer Name Baseball Team's manager: Hall of Famer MILLER Huggins, of course. Skipper of the Cards and Yanks for seventeen seasons, "The Mighty Mite" guided the Yankees to six pennants and three world championships. He's ready and foaming to go!

Not a bad team, eh? Bring on your All-Free Agent Team, your West Virginia Panhandle All-time Nine. We're ready. With a team of Buds and Millers and Schaefers and Porters and Stouts, we're the thirst-quenchingest, run-scoringest team around. And as Leo Durocher almost said: "Dry guys finish last."

BEER AND BASEBALL. Beer and baseball have always gone together about as well as beer and a hot day. Real well!

61

Toast of the Town

Toasting — to drink to someone's health or happiness — is a custom that goes back about as far as drinking itself. In fact, it is one of mankind's oldest social customs. Prehistoric tribes are known to have practiced variations of toasting. The ancient Greeks and Romans solemnized their drinking by offering up "good healths" to their numerous gods and to their dead. Norsemen did much the same, saluting Thor, Odin, and Freya.

It wasn't until seventeenth-century England, however, that the word *toast* came into being. In those days beer was often enjoyed near the fireplace, with bits of toasted bread frequently added to the brew for a little extra flavor. Because the addition of the toast was done before imbibing and the wishing of health, wealth, or whatever was likewise done before imbibing, it stands to reason that the name for the latter took its name from that of the former.

Actually there's not really that much reason to the above reasoning at all . . . but words have come to be in far stranger ways, and it is the more or less accepted derivation of "toast."

Regardless of its derivation, toasting is a wonderful custom. Somehow a beer (or

BOTTOMS UP! Bottoms up is a traditional American toast. Traditional toasts from other lands include:
Skoal! (Scandinavian)
Prosit! (German)
Vivat! (Polish)
L'chayim! (Hebrew)
Salute! (Italian)
A Votre Santé! (French)
Salud! (Spanish)
   and that old standby . . .
Za Vashe Zdorovye! (Russian)
(Coaster courtesy F. X. Matt Brewing Co., of Utica, N.Y.)

anything else . . . though I hate to admit it) always seems to taste better if it's drunk to someone or something. To get you going, here are a few of my favorite toasts culled from the thirst-provoking pages of Lewis C. Henry's *Toasts for All Occasions* (Halcyon House, Garden City, New York).

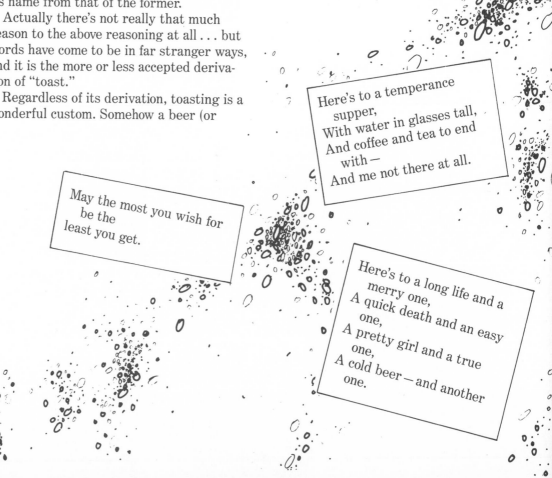

Here's to a temperance supper,
With water in glasses tall,
And coffee and tea to end with —
And me not there at all.

May the most you wish for be the least you get.

Here's to a long life and a merry one,
A quick death and an easy one,
A pretty girl and a true one,
A cold beer — and another one.

May all your labors be in vein.

— *Miner's toast*

Here's to ~~beefsteak~~ chicken legs when you're hungry, ~~Beer~~ Whisky when you're dry, ~~women~~ All the ~~girls~~ you ever want, And heaven when you die.

(... *with corrections by the author!*)

Here's to us that are here, to you that are there, and the rest of us everywhere.

— *Kipling*

May the joys of today
Be those of tomorrow
The goblets of Life
Hold no dregs of sorrow.

— *Estelle Foreman*

May you live all the days of your life.

— *Swift*

Here's to the fellow who smiles
When life runs along like a song,
And here's to the chap who can smile
When everything goes dead wrong.

Continued on next page

DAISY WAS A GOOD OLD DOG. Here's one for all the dog lovers of the world . . . and all the dogs, too: "A Toast for ye Dog" postcard from the early 1900s. The words may be old, but their meaning still rings true.

AWAY ALL EVIL SPIRITS. The clinking of glasses, a custom that goes right along with the offering of a toast, has its origins in early Christian time. It was believed that the making of such a noise would drive away any and all evil spirits that might be lurking in the brew.

ALEXANDRINA, IS THAT YOU? 'Twas considered gallant for a man in Roman times to prove his love was true by drinking a glass of brew for each letter of his fair damsel's name . . . which is what lead, of course, to the well-known Roman proverb:

> If you don't like your brew,
> Stick with a Peg or a Sue.
> If you do like your brew,
> Alexandrina or Christabella . . .
> could be the girl for you.

. . . plus one culled from the thirst-provoking recesses of my brain and dedicated to you, the reader of *From Beer to Eternity*.

A Toast To You

A toast to you
    who enjoys these pages.
A toast to you
    you sage of sages:
May your health be strong,
May your life be long,
And may it always be filled
    with beer, friends, and song.

Ale: A Dish Fit for a King

In *Winter's Tale* Shakespeare wrote, "A quart of ale is a dish fit for a king." And Shakespeare knew what of he spoke: his father was an ale conner, an official taster of ale who had the authority to condemn a bad batch or order it to be sold at a lower price if it were not up to standard.

Ale, more or less *the* drink of the British Isles, differs from its cousin, lager, in several major respects. It has a more pronounced hop flavor, tastes more bitter or tart, is generally more full-bodied, and very often has a higher alcoholic content. True ales are top fermented—as opposed to lagers, which are bottom fermented—but there are plenty of untrue (i.e., bottom fermented) ales that taste mighty fine and that would please all but the harshest of ale enthusiasts. Porter and stout are both types of ale.

KING ME!

Discover the daring, distinctive, discriminating, delicious taste of Little Kings Cream Ale... and you'll say "KING ME"!

THE SCHOENLING BREWING COMPANY, Cincinnati, Ohio

KING ME! Ale comes in an amazing assortment of varieties. One variety that has its following in America is cream ale, so called because its relatively high level of carbonation leads to a hearty, rich foam. Genesee, Utica Club, and Liebotschaner cream ales all have their advocates in the East, while Little Kings, a product of Cincinnati's Hudepohl-Schoenling Brewing Company, has swept away many a taste bud throughout the heartland. (Courtesy Hudepohl-Schoenling Brewing Company)

"Oh Be Jolly!"

P.B. ALE
Reg. U. S. Pat. Off.

A Most Convincing Ale

"*It's the best ale I ever drank.*"

That's the invariable comment of the man who takes his first bottle of **P. B. Ale**.

P. B. Ale is a "mighty convincing" ale. It's the best ale brewed in any country. The man who knows when **ale is ale** recognizes **P. B.** as the real thing.

The best appetizer and digestive with Lobster and Welsh Rabbit.

Just as good with chop or steak.

Tip the waiter off to serve you P. B. Ale.

In bottle or on draught at all leading Hotels, Restaurants and Cafes.

SUPPLIED BY PARK & TILFORD, New York, CLEMES & O'BRIEN CO., N. Y., C. JEVNE & CO., Chicago, S. S. PIERCE CO., Boston, and first-class Grocers.

BUNKER HILL BREWERIES
Charlestown, Mass.

New York Office   42 East 23d St.

"OH BE JOLLY!" New England has traditionally been an ale stronghold in the States. One of the breweries that satisfied the thirst of that stronghold for close to sixty years (1860–1918) was the Van Nostrand Bunker Hill Breweries located in Charlestown, Massachusetts. Here's a wonderful 1907 advertisement for their P. B. Ale.

> "Fill with mingled cream and amber
> I will dram that glass again.
> Such hilarious visions clamber
> Through the chamber of my brain—
> Quaintest thoughts—queerest fancies
> Come to life and fade away:
> Who cares how time advances?
> I am drinking ale today."
> —*Edgar Allan Poe, 1848*

The Brewing Fraternity: The Names You Love to Drink

Hail, hail the gang's all here. Or most of them anyway. Getting a bunch of busy brewers together for a group photo is difficult indeed, but we've done it. Here, together for the first time, are most of the guys responsible for the names you love to drink. The problem is, though, that even when you finally do get them together, they're a restless lot, looking this way and that. And they're not big on smiling. Come on guys, loosen up a little!

Peter Ballantine: Born in Mauchline, Ayershire, Scotland in November 1791. Came to America in 1820. Worked at a

tavern in Black Rock, Connecticut, before moving to Troy, New York, working there in the local ale brewery. Lived up to Scottish thriftiness by saving his pennies, moving across the Hudson to Albany in the early 1830s, and starting his own brewery. Desiring to be closer to the rich New York market, he moved to Newark in 1840. Brewed only ale until 1879, when an entirely new operation was begun for the manufacture of lager. Died in 1883.

Valentin Blatz: Born in Miltenberg-on-the-Main, Bavaria, in October 1826, the son of a brewer. Came to America in 1849, stopping briefly in Buffalo before settling in

Milwaukee. Worked in a small brewery operated by John Braun for two years, saving his money so he could become his own master, which he did in 1851. Credited with being, in 1875, the first Milwaukee brewer to bottle beer.

Anton Blitz: Purchased the four-year-old Portland Brewing Co., of Portland, Oregon, in 1909. Operated it until Prohibition and had enough faith during the dry years to rebuild almost the entire plant. Merged with rival Henry Weinhard to form Blitz-Weinhard in 1928.

Adolphus Busch: Born in 1839 in Kastell, Germany, the youngest of twenty-one children. Came to America in 1857, establishing himself in the brewer's supply business in St. Louis. Married Eberhard Anheuser's daughter Lilly in 1861, becoming a partner in the brewery in 1865. Oversaw the success of Budweiser, introduced in 1876, and the tremendous growth of Anheuser-Busch into the most powerful brewery in the nation. Died in 1913.

Adolph Coors: Born in Prussia. Arriving in America as a stowaway in 1868, he was apprehended and almost sent back to Germany. He pledged to find work to pay for the cost of passage, however, and was allowed to remain. Founded, with Jacob

Left to right: J. Schlitz, F. Pabst, D.G. Yuengling, A. Schell, F. Miller, A. Busch, C. Schmidt, C. Moerlein, C. Stegmaier, V. Blatz, G. Wiedemann, H. Weinhard, L. Hudepohl. Camera Shy: J. Schmidt, F.X. Matt, G., M., and W. Piel, M. Schaefer, J. Leinenkugel, A. Coors, P. Straub, A. Blitz, G. Heileman, P. Ballantine, F. Schaefer, B. Stroh, and T. Hamm.

Continued on next page

A happy New Year
1889.
Ph Best Brewing Co

Ph. BEST
BREWING CO
MILWAUKEE.WIS.

1889

"A Happy New Year, 1889" message from the Phillip Best Brewing Company. It would be the company's last. Later in the year it would become the Pabst Brewing Co.

The Bests

The name "Best" is not one you'll find among our brewing fraternity. That's because there is no American beer called Best today. Yet both of today's Milwaukee brewing giants had their origin as "Bests" in the very same Best family.

In 1844 Jacob Best founded what would (in 1889) become the Pabst Brewing Company. Six years later, in 1850, two of his sons, Charles and Lorenz Best, established the Menomonee Valley Brewery. Also known as the Plank Road Brewery, we know it today as the Miller Brewing Company.

Although present-day Miller policy is to play down their historical relationship with the Best family — no mention of it is included in the company's booklet, *The Miller Legacy* — Pabst follows a different route. To this day, almost a hundred years after the company name was changed to Pabst, there is still a "B" — for Best — included on every Pabst label.

Schueler, the Golden Brewery in 1873. Start-up costs totaled but twenty thousand dollars, with Schueler putting up eighteen thousand of it. The firm was known as Schueler & Coors until 1880, when Coors bought full control. Died in a freak accident — he fell out of a sixth-floor hotel room while recovering from a bout of the flu — in 1929.

Theodore Hamm: born in Baden, Germany, in 1825. Came to America in 1854, first finding employ in his trade of butcher in Buffalo and Chicago. In 1856 he moved to St. Paul, where he operated a boarding house and saloon before purchasing the small brewery of A. F. Keller in 1865. Under his direction the brewery grew to be the largest industry in St. Paul. Often called Bruderle Hamm — little brother — by his friends and employees, Hamm formed

the first labor union in St. Paul for the benefit of his employees.

Gottlieb Heileman: Born in Wurttemberg, Germany, in 1822. Was a brewer and baker in his homeland until, frustrated at not achieving master brewer status, he left for America in 1848. Took up baking in partnership with Gottlieb Maier in Milwaukee, but brewing ran deep in his soul. Selling his share of the bakery to Maier for $1,520, Heileman moved to LaCrosse and entered into a brewing partnership with John Gund. That was 1858. Fourteen years later Gund left the firm to form his own brewery, leaving Heileman sole owner of the newly renamed Gottlieb Heileman City Brewery. Died in 1876.

Louis Hudepohl: Born in Cincinnati in July 1842. Real name was Ludwig, but Americanized it to Louis. Practiced trade

T. Hamm

Stoney's

From Ballantine to Yuengling all the names included here are last names ... a throwback to the early days of American merchandising, when a person's output was very apt to be known simply by his or her last name. Made-up names — a la Rheingold, Budweiser, or Iron City — were a rather rare exception. If Joe Doak produced pickles, they'd likely be called Doak's Pickles; if Joe Doak produced beer, it'd likely be called Doak's Beer. They would not be called Joe's Pickles or Joe's Beer.

There is one yet-with-us beer, however, that does take its name from a brewer's first name, or rather his nickname for his first name. That's Stoney's Beer, the pride of the Jones Brewing Company of Smithton, Pennsylvania. Before Prohibition the then-named Eureka Brewing Company sold its beer under the name Eureka Gold Crown. During Prohibition they shifted to ice and near beer ... and somehow Stoney, the nickname of company founder and president Wiliam B. Jones, took hold. People began asking for Stoney's Near Beer. Going with the flow, the company organized a Stoney Jones baseball team that traveled up and down the Monongahela Valley further spreading the name. When beer came back in 1933, it just seemed natural to stick with the Stoney's ... and so it has been ever since.

WILLIAM B. "STONEY" JONES. Born in Wales in 1874. Came to America in 1885 and found work as a coal miner in the area southeast of Pittsburgh. In 1900 he acquired the Smithton Hotel in Smithton. Through his ownership of the hotel he became familiar with the brewing industry, and in 1905 he decided to build his own brewery. The Eureka Brewing Company opened in the fall of 1907. Stoney Jones lived through Prohibition ... and to see his name in lights and on signs and labels, too. He died in 1936. (Courtesy Jones Brewing Co.)

LOOKING GOOD. The Stoney Jones baseball team as it appeared in 1923. (Courtesy Jones Brewing Co.)

of wholesaling surgical instruments; later the wholesaling of liquors. In partnership with George H. Kotte, purchased the Koehler Brewery in 1885. Expanded the operation until it had over one hundred employees in 1890 and production was forty thousand barrels a year. Became Hudepohl Brewing Co. in 1899. Died at his home in Cincinnati in 1902.

Jacob Leinenkugel: Born in Germany in 1842. Came to America at the age of three when his father, Matthias, moved the family to Sauk City, Wisconsin, in order to found a brewery. Matthias sired five sons and each went on to found his own brewery. Jacob founded his, with partner John Miller, in Chippewa Falls in 1867. In 1884 he

Continued on next page

bought out Miller, becoming sole proprietor of Jacob Leinenkugel's Spring Brewery. The "Spring" was dropped in 1898. Today the brewery is simply the Jacob Leinenkugel Brewing Company. Jacob died in 1899.

F. X. (Francis Xavier) Matt: Born in Germany in 1859. Learned the art of brewing at the Duke of Boden's brewery in Rothaus, Germany, before coming to America in 1878. Associated himself with Charles Bierbauer's Brewery in Utica and became the brewery's superintendent upon Bierbauer's death in 1885. Changed the firm's name to the West End Brewing Co. in 1888 and successfully guided it for the next sixty-two years, until his retirement in 1950. The brewery is today known as the F. X. Matt Brewing Company.

Frederic Miller: A native of Germany, where he learned his brewing early, he rose to the position of brewmaster to the Royal Court at Hohenzollern Castle. Came to America in 1854 for political and personal reasons. Traveled through much of America for a full year before selecting Milwaukee as his brewery site. In 1855 purchased the already-established Menomonee Valley Brewery, also known as the Plank Road Brewery. Produced but three hundred barrels of beer in his first year of operation, but had seen that multiply many times over — to eighty thousand barrels a year — by the time of his death in 1888.

Christian Moerlein: Born in Truppach, Bavaria, in May 1818. As a child, learned both his father's trade of blacksmithing and his uncle's of brewing. Came to America in 1841. Settled in Cincinnati in 1842, establishing a successful blacksmith shop. Became increasingly convinced that brewing offered more promise and in 1853 established a small brewery in partnership with Adam Dillman. Was later in partnership with Conrad Windisch before becoming sole proprietor in 1866. Died in 1895.

Frederick Pabst: Born in Nicholausreith, Saxony, Germany, in March 1836. Came to America as a twelve-year-old with his family in 1848. His mother passed away the

EBERHARD ANHEUSER. Half of his daughters (two out of four) married Buschs.

The Joy of Marriage

Marrying the boss's daughter — or widow — is a time-honored tradition. Ask our brewing fraternity . . . they know.

Frederick Pabst married Marie Best, daughter of Phillip Best and granddaughter of brewery founder Jacob Best, in 1862. Within two years he'd traded in his Great Lakes steamer days for a partnership in Phillip's brewery.

Adolphus Busch married Lilly Anheuser, one of the four daughters of struggling St. Louis brewer Eberhard Anheuser, in 1861. In fact it was a double wedding. Adolphus's older brother Ulrich married Lilly's sister Anna as part of the same ceremony. Four years later, in 1865, Adolphus became a partner in the brewery. For a more complete rundown of the Busch-Anheuser union, see page 153.

When brewer August Krug died in 1856, his trusty bookkeeper, Joseph Schlitz, stepped in and took over the management of the firm. At some point, exactly when seems to be lost in the annals of time, Joseph also stepped in and married Krug's widow. Alas they both drowned while on a trip to Germany in 1875.

Last but not least is Valentin Blatz. He worked in the Milwaukee brewery of John Braun for two years, until he went out and founded his own small brewhouse in 1851. Later that same year, however, Braun died. Val put aside his own tiny operation, married Braun's widow, and acquired his former boss's brewery.

very next year, and young Frederick was forced to go to work in a hotel at a salary of five dollars a month. Later he secured employment on a Great Lakes steamer, where he advanced rapidly. By the time he was twenty-one, he was Captain Frederick Pabst, skipper of the steamer "Huron." In 1862 the captain married Marie Best, daughter of successful Milwaukee brewer Phillip Best. Pabst gave up his nautical career to become a partner in the brewery in 1864. By 1889 Pabst was in sole control of the firm and changed its name to the Pabst Brewing Co. He died in 1904.

Gottfried, Michael, and Wilhelm Piel: Brothers from the Dusseldorf area of Germany who came to America sometime during 1882 or 1883. In 1883 they combined their resources and bought a small brewery in the East New York section of Brooklyn, selling most of their output on premises during the early years. The brothers were innovators. Piel's was the first brewery in America to use colored glass bottles to better protect their beer. They were also among the first in the country to use an automatic pasteurizer. Michael died in 1915; Gottfried in 1935.

Frederick Schaefer: Born in Wetzlar, Prussia in 1817. Came to America in 1838, arriving in New York with exactly one dollar to his name. Within two weeks, however, he was gainfully employed in the Manhattan brewery of Sebastian Sommers. Together with younger brother Maximilian, saved and scrimped, and in 1842 was able to buy out Sommers. Oversaw the brewery's move to new and larger quarters several times. Died in 1896.

Maximilian Schaefer: Born in Wetzler, Prussia. Came to America in 1839, bringing with him a formula for lager beer. Teamed up with older brother Frederick to buy the small brewery of Sebastian Sommers in 1842 and to start brewing lager for New York's beer drinkers. Witnessed the move of the brewery "uptown" to Fourth (now Park) Avenue and Fifty-first Street, the present site of St. Bartholomew's Church,

in 1849. Outlived his brother and ran the brewery until his own death in 1904.

August Schell: Born in Durback, Baden, Germany, in 1828. Came to America just before mid-century, eventually settling in New Ulm, Minnesota, in 1856. A machinist by trade, he worked in that capacity for the flour mills operated by the German Land Association before branching out into brewing in 1860. Surviving Indian attacks and Minnesota's rigorous winters, Schell slowly but surely built his brewery into a successful venture. He died in 1891.

Joseph Schlitz: Born in Mayence, Germany, in May 1831. Came to America in 1855, finding work as a bookkeeper in the Milwaukee brewery of August Krug. Krug died in 1856, and Schlitz assumed management of the company. He also married Krug's widow. In 1874, the brewery's name was changed to the Jos. Schlitz Brewing Co. Unfortunately Schlitz didn't have much of a chance to savor the name change. He died in a drowning accident while on a trip back to his native Germany the very next year, 1875.

Christian Schmidt: Born in Machstadt, Wurttemberg, Germany, in 1832. He founded his Philadelphia brewery in 1860. In spite of being German, Schmidt's original output was limited to ale and porter. Lager was not added until 1880. He died in 1895.

Jacob Schmidt: Born in Bavaria in 1845. Learned the trade of brewing in his native land before coming to America in 1865. Worked in breweries in Rochester, Milwaukee, and Minnesota before settling permanently in St. Paul, purchasing a half-interest in a brewery there in 1884. Lived to see the brewery become the Jacob Schmidt Brewing Co. in 1900. Died in 1911.

Charles Stegmaier: Born in Wurttemberg, Germany, in October 1831. Practiced brewing from age fifteen in his homeland. Came to America in 1849; moved to Wilkes-Barre two years later. He formed a partnership with John Reichard in 1851 to begin a brewery. Credited with being the first to

F. Schaefer

Continued on next page

71

brew lager in northeastern Pennsylvania. Later went out on his own to found what became the largest brewery in Pennsylvania outside of Philadelphia and Pittsburgh. Died in 1906.

Peter Straub: A Bavarian by birth and a cooper by trade, Peter Straub founded a small brewery in the wilds of north central Pennsylvania in 1872. Today third and fourth generation Straubs run the brewery, still small by any standard of measurement. Sales are about twenty thousand barrels a year, most of it sold right in St. Mary's and surrounding Elk County.

Bernard Stroh: Born in Germany in 1822. Set out for the "New World" while in his twenties. At first planned to settle in Brazil but realized opportunities were far greater in America. Took a liking to Detroit and founded a small brewery, called the Lion Brewery, there in 1850. It had become the largest brewery in Michigan by the time Stroh passed away in 1882.

Henry Weinhard: born in Lindenbronn, Wurttemberg, Germany, in February 1830. Learned the brewing trade as a youth. Came to America in 1851, working in breweries in Philadelphia, St. Louis, Cincinnati, and other locales before striking out for

B. Stroh

the West Coast in 1856. With him were his German brewmaster papers and a hand-made copper brew kettle. Set up operations in Fort Vancouver (now Vancouver), Washington, for a number of years before moving to Portland, Oregon, for good in 1862.

George Wiedemann: Born in Saxony, Germany. Came to America in 1853, settling in Cincinnati after brief stays in Brooklyn and Louisville. Associated himself with several breweries in "The Queen City of the Ohio" until 1870, when he joined forces with John Butcher, who was operating a tiny fifteen-barrels-a-day brewhouse in Newport, Kentucky. In 1878 Weidemann became sole proprietor. He constructed a modern plant in 1888. Died in 1890.

David G. Yuengling: Born in Germany in 1806. Came to America in 1828 and, attracted by the pure mountain spring water of Pottsville, Pennsylvania, founded a brewery there the very next year, 1829. A fire destroyed the original brewery in 1831 but, undaunted, Yuengling just built a new and better one. he obviously built it to last, too. Today, 111 years after David Yuengling's death in 1876, his firm still lives on . . . America's oldest continuously operated brewery.

You Vill Drink Beer

"**M**y people must drink beer. His majesty was brought up on beer and so were his ancestors and his officers and soldiers. Many battles have been fought and won by soldiers nourished on beer, and the King does not believe that coffee-drinking soldiers can be depended on to endure hardships or to beat the enemies."

*—Frederick the Great,
King of Prussia, September 13, 1777*

From Beer to Ballet

A goodly portion of the John F. Kennedy Center for the Performing Arts in Washington, D.C., was the site, from 1872 to 1956, of the Chr. Heurich Brewing Co. After their brewing days were done, the Heurich family donated the land to the center.

Chr. Heurich, the last operating brewery in the nation's capital, was headed by one man for a remarkable sixty-seven years. That man, of course, was Christian Heurich. In 1872 he took over the brewery that bore his name and ran it until his death — at the well-lagered age of 103 — in 1945. At the time he was characterized as the "oldest active employee in the world." And that he undoubtedly was!

The Family Mansion, Too

Washington has done extremely well by the Heurichs. Not only did the family deed the brewery site to the JFK Center for the Performing Arts, they donated the family mansion to the Columbia Historical Society, which uses it to house their most impressive collection of items from the city's past.

The John F. Kennedy Center as it appears today. (Photo courtesy The John F. Kennedy Center for the Performing Arts)

FULL LINE. As with so many old-time breweries. Chr. Heurich was proud of their full line of brews. The labels pictured here give an idea of their after-repeal output.

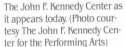

73

Stout: Dark, Strong, and Sweet

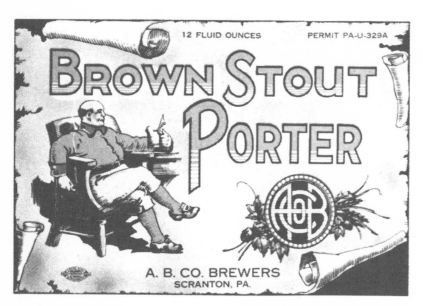

THROWBACK. A throwback to stout's early stout porter days in England is this circa 1935 label for Brown Stout Porter. It was brewed — brown and strong — by Scranton's A. B. Co. from 1933 to 1937.

Stout is a type of ale, similar to porter, but with a darker color, a stronger and sweeter taste, and a hoppier flavor. Legend has it that it was originally called stout porter in honor of a select group of English porters who could carry only the very heaviest of loads.

A favorite in Ireland (Guinness!), England, and the former British islands of the West Indies, stout has never won many popularity awards in America. A lot of it goes down a lot of throats on, naturally enough, St. Patrick's Day, but consumption the rest of the year is but a drop in the total U.S. beer picture.

Stout is good stuff, though, especially when either very cold or, ironically, very warm weather calls for something more bracing than the norm. Look for England's Mackeson's, Jamaica's Dragon, and of course Ireland's Guinness. Or look a little harder and you *may* find U.S.-brewed stout. Several of the micros brew it and with enough requests hopefully others will, too.

GOOD. A bottle of Sierra Nevada Stout moments before being consumed by the author. It was *good*. Sierra Nevada is brewed by the Sierra Nevada Brewing Company, Chico, California, one of a handful of micros presently brewing stout for the American market.

GOOD OLD GLIX. Relatively few U.S. brewers have tried their hand at stout. One that did was the Grand Valley Brewing Co. of Ionia, Michigan, brewing up Glix Stout from 1933 to 1937. Sales were disappointing.

Oh My Gosh, It's Miss Frothingslosh!

Big on beauty.
Big on talent.
Big on enthusiasm.
Big.
That's Miss Frothingslosh!

Miss Frothingslosh was the product of fertile minds at the Pittsburgh Brewing Company, but Olde Frothingslosh—the beer that spawned Miss F—was the product of the fertile mind of Rege Cordic, one of the zaniest radio personalities ever to enliven Steel City airwaves. Rege invented Olde Frothingslosh in 1954 as a gag, part of one of his crazy routines.

It was a gag that tickled the fancy of the brewery. They decided to have some fun, too. They took several hundred cases of their regular Iron City Beer, put comical Olde Frothingslosh ("The Pale Stale Ale with the Foam on the Bottom") labels on it, and gave it away as Christmas gifts to friends and business associates of the brewery.

What started as a gag because it tickled the fancy of a couple of folks at Pittsburgh Brewing, however, tickled a lot of other fancies, too. People liked Olde Frothingslosh

and they bought it, so the brewery kept on marketing it.

In 1969, to add yet more zany zest to Olde Frothingslosh's sales effort, Miss Frothingslosh was brought on the scene, and when she arrived, she arrived! Selected as the winner in a Miss Frothingslosh Beauty Contest, Miss F was, in real life, a former go-go dancer (honest!); but in the world of western Pennsylvania beer, she was Miss Frothingslosh, aka Fatima Yechburgh.

Since 1969 Fatima has graced several Olde Frothingslosh cans and has been starred on her very own calendar, but her specialty, not awfully surprisingly, has been in-person appearances. When Miss F, at 250 robust pounds, appears in person, there's quite frankly a lot of person that's doing the appearing. She's especially in demand at beer can collectors' conventions. Commented her husband, Norman: "Here [around Pittsburgh] we go shopping and nobody recognizes us. When we go to beer can conventions, we have to have security guards. Martha's real big at those things."

Real big!

LOOKING GOOD. Miss Frothingslosh as she appeared in her beer can debut in 1969 . . .

. . . . and looking sweet and lovely on the pier. Quips the brewery: Fatima's big on health . . . . She's been building up her body for years. (Photo courtesy Pittsburgh Brewing Company)

"THE ONLY BREW YOU CAN FIND IN THE DARK." Typical, wacky Olde Frothingslosh label. "Distributed thru Electric Outlets." Ouch!

The Charge of the Microbrewery Brigade

Without any doubt the most exciting thing happening in U.S. beer in the 1980s is the microbrewery movement. It's almost like American brewing 150 years ago: very small, very local brewers producing distinctive, almost handmade brews.

The movement was more or less spearheaded in the 1970s by an American sailor named Jack McAuliffe. McAuliffe, stationed in Scotland, was most impressed with the richness, the character, the taste of the malty Scottish ales that were everywhere around him. His only problem: his service pay didn't afford him enough coin to enjoy the brews as often as he wanted, so he decided to try brewing them himself. The results weren't bad . . . and when he returned home to America, he kept on home brewing. Eventually he decided to share the wealth with others by going commercial. The result,

in 1977, was the New Albion Brewing Co. located in Sonoma, California.

Sad to say, after six years of brewing success—if not financial success—New Albion folded in 1983. Jack McAuliffe's pioneering influence, however, lives on . . . very nicely. Commented William O'Shea, executive secretary of the Brewers' Association of America: "All of a sudden I'm getting calls from people all over the country wanting information about starting small, family-type breweries. Its impact on the beer industry is minuscule at this point, but the trend is refreshing."

Mr. O'Shea, you've said a mouthful. All types of ales, porters, stouts, rich lagers, weiss beers, even barley wines are now available. Yep, refreshing is very definitely the right word!

SMALL. Micros aren't called micros for nothing. For instance, the Chesapeake Bay Brewing Co., opened in 1980, has a yearly capacity of 4,500 barrels . . . more or less what Anheuser-Busch brews in a half hour.

Chesapeake Bay Brewing Co., Virginia Beach, Virginia

DROPS IN THE BUCKET. Over forty American micros have opened for business in the last decade. Most are still at it. Although their output represents but drops in the total U.S. beer bucket, they're rich, hearty drops.

SIERRA NEVADA CELEBRATION ALE

BREWED AND BOTTLED BY SIERRA NEVADA BREWING CO.
CHICO CALIFORNIA
NET CONTENTS 12 FL. OZ.

MASH TUN
BREW HAUS
HOT
HOT WATER TANK
BOILER

BOULDER PORTER
BOULDER BREWING CO. BOULDER, COLO.
12 FL. OZ.
355 ML

PALO BILL'S BREW PUB
HAYWARD, CALIFORNIA
BEER
Barley, Hops, W
1 PINT 8

COLLIN COUNTY PURE GOLD BEER
HAND BREWED AND BOTTLED
BY REINHEITSGEBOT BREWING COMPANY
PLANO, TEXAS
12 FL. OZ.

Chesbay
a superior lager beer

BREWED AND BO
PALO ALTO BR
MOUNTAIN VIEW, C

355 ml.
12 fl. oz.
Ingredients: Water, Malted Barley, Hops & Yeast
Caldwell, Idaho 83605
Brewed and Bottled in Idaho
Amber Lager

EN BEAR
12 FL. OZ.
Purest
Ingredients

THOMAS EMPER
E BEER

Finest Quality

SIERRA NEVADA. PORTER
This Porter is entirely handmade, in the "old world" tradition, using the finest barley malts, whole hops, brewers yeast and water.
AND BOTTLED BY SIERRA NEVADA BREWING CO., CHICO, CALIF. ©198
NET CONTENTS 12 FL. OZ.

California

NEW AMSTERDAM AMBER BEER
12 fl. oz.

GEMÜTLICHKEIT
KÜFNERBRÄU
OLD BAVARIAN STYLE BEER
11 Fl. Oz. Brewed by Küfnerbräu Montoe, WA

PYRAMID ALES

77

Say, Buddy, Can You Spare 5¢, 10¢, 25¢, 50¢, $1.00, $2.00, $3.00?

Beer is certainly still the popular-priced drink, but when a bottle of Rolling Rock costs me $3.00, as it did the other day in a posh (translation: stuffy and overpriced!) pub in Manhattan, I begin to wonder what it's all coming to. So before we hit $5.00 for a beer, here's a longing look back at the seems-like-just-yesteryear days of 5¢ and 10¢ beers. Where have you gone, Joe Dimaggio?

YES, SIR, MR. PRESIDENT. In 1947 President Truman asked the nation to cut prices. This Queens, New York, tavern pitched right in by lowering their beer a healthy 10 percent... from 10¢ a glass all the way down to 9¢ a glass.

To restore public confidence; aid in relieving unemployment; help bring back normalcy and general countrywide prosperity, we believe that

This Country Needs a Good 5 Cent Glass of Beer

PUBLIC CONFIDENCE, UNEMPLOYMENT, PROSPERITY... AT 5¢ A GLASS. Circa 1932 postcard championing the repeal of Prohibition and the return of nickel beer and prosperity.

ROPKINS & CO.

232 to 242 SHELDON ST., Hartford, Conn.

TELEPHONE 1677.

BREWERS AND BOTTLERS OF

Ales and Porter

(exclusively.)

SPECIAL BREWINGS which we bottle for HOUSEHOLD USE, DELIVERED to any part of the city FREE:

Ropkins' BITTER ALE,   · $1.25 per doz. pts.
Ropkins' LIGHT DINNER ALE, .60   "
Ropkins' FAMILY PORTER, · .65   "
Ropkins' STOCK PORTER, · 1.00   "

DELIVERED, NO LESS. 1906 ad for the ales and porters of Hartford's Ropkins & Company. It doesn't take a math wizard to figure out that, at 60¢ the dozen pints, the Light Dinner Ale works out to 5¢ a pint. For 25¢ you could've had quite a dinner!

PRICE WAR. 5¢ a glass is fine... but 3¢ a large stein is even finer. This bargain of bargains was the result of a May 1933 price war between a couple of rival Chicago bars.

OLD VIENNA . . . 6 FOR 87¢.
Late 1960s "let's-put-the-price-right-on-the-can" can from Los Angeles' Maier Brewing Co. How good was Old Vienna? At six for 87¢, it was just fine!

"FULL 12 OZS." 10¢ a bottle and three for 25¢ was fairly standard pricing in the late 1940s . . . even for a more-expensive-to-brew all-malt beer like Trommer's White Label.

LET'S ALL DRINK TO THAT. Nickel beer made one of its increasingly infrequent comebacks in March 1949. The place to be was Sam Atkins's Bar and Grill at 79 St. Mark's Place in New York's East Village. Here barmaid Helen Johnson joins in the joy as she scoops it up at 5¢ a good-sized glass. (Photo courtesy *New York News*)

TIMES CHANGE. This is 79 St. Mark's Place as it looked in 1985. Nickel beer is gone; Helen Johnson is gone; Sam Atkins's customers are gone; Sam Atkins's Bar and Grill is gone. Where have you gone, Sam Atkins?

MORAL: Is there a moral to all this? If there is, it would be: better enjoy your beer now . . . before prices go up again!

Breweriana

Turn-of-the-century blob top bottle from the days when F. & M. Schaefer was located on Fifty-first Street and Fourth (now Park) Avenue in Manhattan. Schaefer moved to Brooklyn in 1916 and sold their site on Park Avenue to St. Bartholomew's Church. St. Bart's is still there to this day.

Breweriana is a word — *the* word — that describes any and all beer advertising and packaging . . . and that runs quite a gamut. Included are beer signs, trays, bottles, cans, coasters, labels, mugs, glasses, ads, tap knobs, openers, etc., etc., etc. The list is almost endless . . . just about anything and everything that pertains to beer but the beer itself.

Why People Collect Breweriana

In attempting to explain the then fledging fascination of breweriana, I penned the following stirring words as part of the introduction to *Beers, Breweries & Breweriana*, written in 1969. I think they still hold true today.

People collect things for different reasons. Generally, however, these reasons revolve around either or both of two core motives — fun or profit. To our way of thinking, breweriana collecting fulfills both of these goals very nicely.

For the Fun of It

First of all, the American brewing industry has had a fascinating history. Going way back to the early days of our country, most every household was a "brewery" in the same sense that each was also a "bakery" and a "farm." People were pretty much self-sufficient and malt beverages were home-brewed. By the middle 1800s, however, most malt beverages were commercially brewed. This can be shown by the fact that in 1850 there were 431 commercial breweries in the United States, as compared with only 129 in 1810. In 1860 there were 1,261, and by 1879–80 this figure had risen to a remarkable 2,520. Those were the days when most every town of any consequence (except in the South) had its own brewery and its own beer. And what could be more fascinating? Almost regardless of where you live, it is possible to ferret out facts about and items from local breweries — whether "local" means a particular town, a particular state, or even a particular group of states.

However, equally as much fun as a "local" collection is the converse — a collection representing brands and breweries from all over the country (or even the world, for that matter). Beer, unlike most mass-produced items, has had few national brands. This, of course, was especially true before the great rise in packaged beer sales following repeal, but it is even true today. Even such very well known brands as Coors, Falstaff, Lucky Lager, Rheingold, Schaefer, etc., are not distributed nationally. And just try getting Point Special outside of the Wisconsin-Illinois area or Shriner outside of central Texas. As a result, a business or pleasure trip is a lot more interesting — whether you're a bottle or tray collector stopping at antique shops and flea markets or a can collector stopping at bars, grocery and liquor stores!

As an Investment

In addition to the fun of collecting it, breweriana appears to be a good investment. The prices of antiques in general have risen considerably over the past few years, and this seems to be especially true with the newer types of Americana — items from the turn-of-the-century up through the mid 1940s.

Breweriana definitely fits in the last category, and the price for trays and signs has risen astronomically in some areas of the country. This may in part be due to the greatly increased interest in old advertising items to decorate home bars, dens, and playrooms. Restaurants and tap rooms decorated in the 1890s style have also increased demand. However, the basic reason is, naturally, the great increase in private collecting. With an ever increasing amount of leisure time, more people are channeling more and more of their spare time (and money) into hobbies of all kinds, and, for reasons outlined above, breweriana collecting offers many attractions.

Yep, all these years later those words written in 1969 still hold true. Although at that time I could attempt to list every major breweriana collector in the country within the space of five pages in the back of the book (some sixty-six collectors were included), today it would take a telephone book–sized volume to attempt to accomplish the same thing. Since the early 1970s breweriana collecting has been a hot hobby!

Colorful

It's almost a crime to show these items in black and white . . . most of them are so very colorful. On the other hand, it's probably just as well. If they were in color they'd most likely steal the show from the rest of the book . . . and that would be a no-no because *From Beer to Eternity* isn't meant to be just about breweriana; it's meant to be about all aspects of the wonder of beer.

Further Insights

For further insights into breweriana collecting and collectors, see Mr. Budman (page 148), The Hamm's Man of the Midwest (page 48), Tribute to a Breweriana Pioneer (page 24), and Where It All Happens: Macungie, Pennsylvania (page 132).

Circa 1950 "Burger Please" ad from Cincinnati's Burger Brewing Co. Burger went out of business in 1973, but the name lives on as a brand that is still brewed by the Hudepohl-Schoenling Brewing Co.

Breweriana comes in all sizes and shapes. Here's a lineup that includes a milk glass-type sign from the Gluek Brewing Co. of Minneapolis (1857-1965); an early-1900s ad from Boston's Massachusetts Breweries Company (1901-18); a uniform patch from when the Iroquois Brewing Co. (1892-1971) was still brewing away in Buffalo; a barrel-shaped half-gallon bottle from San Francisco's Globe Brewing Co. (1933-38); an early squat blob Philadelphia Porter & Ale bottle; a quart spout top can from the Fox DeLuxe Brewing Co., Grand Rapids, Michigan (1941-51); a pre-Prohibition bottle from Sacramento's storied Buffalo Brewing Co. (1890-1949); a striking girl-and-her-horse oval tray from the Lykens Brewing Company of Lykens, Pennsylvania (1895-1917); and, last but not least, a metal "Blatz on Draft" sign from Milwaukee's Blatz Brewing Co. (1851-1958).

Part of the romance of collecting breweriana undoubtedly stems from the industry's exceedingly high past mortality rate. All of these items, for example, are from breweries that have gone to that happy (or should it be hoppy?!) hunting ground in the sky (although, in some cases, the names live on). There's something especially alluring about collecting items that, no matter how plentiful they may once have been, will never be made again. It's a knowledge that you're preserving a piece of beauty from the past.

Continued on next page

Breweriana, Continued

Back in 1906 you could call Bushwick 267 for a case or two of the Frank Brewery's lager, ale, or porter. Frank was one of more than thirty breweries then in operation in Brooklyn. Today there is none.

Large pre-Prohibition crockery jug from New Bedford's Smith Bros. Brewing Co. Smith Bros. played it both ways: they were wholesale liquor dealers as well as brewers.

Breweriana Clubs

Four major breweriana collectors' clubs have been formed in the past two decades.

- The Beer Can Collectors of America (BCCA) was formed in St. Louis in April 1970 by six can buffs who felt there was joy to the can itself, over and above what was in it.
- The Eastern Coast Breweriana Association (ECBA) was formally established in Hicksville, New York, in September of the same year.
- In January 1972 the National Association of Breweriana Advertising (NABA) was formed in Wisconsin.
- Ten years later, in 1982, the last major club, the American Breweriana Association (ABA), was founded in Boulder, Colorado.

Each club publishes a periodic newsletter/journal with respect to what's happening in the hobby, and each has get-togethers where breweriana buffs meet, buy/sell/trade for their collection, socialize . . . and just plain have a good time.

For membership information on each of these clubs, see page 157.

A good-looking set of 1940s-1950s cans from the Chr. Heurich Brewing Co. (1872-1956), the last active brewery in our nation's capital.

Brewing Beer That Has "Legs": An Interview with Brew Pub Pioneer Buffalo Bill Owens

Brew pubs are blossoming. Long popular in England, the concept of drinking beer brewed right on the premises is now proving to have considerable appeal for Americans as well.

To find out more about what's happening in the world of brew pubs, we spoke to a man who knows . . . one of the pioneers of the American brew pub movement, Buffalo Bill Owens, proprietor of Buffalo Bill's Brewery and Brew Pub, Hayward, California.

Bill, just what is a brew pub?
A brew pub is a bar that brews and sells its beer directly to the customer. In other words, you sit at the bar — and in my place you can look off to your right — and through the window you can see the brewery. And I don't do off-sales. There's no liquor [or grocery] store handling my product. It's all sold right here on premises. I'm a six-barrel brewery, producing 180 gallons a week. That comes out to 320 barrels a year.

What would you say is advantageous about a brew pub from a customer's point of view?
It's the beer. It's unpasteurized and unfiltered. It has legs; it has taste. By legs I mean it'll stand up and walk out of the glass. It's *thick*, will stick to the palate. That it's unpasteurized and unfiltered is also very critical to the taste of the product. Pasteurization kills beer.

You're copyrighting — or trying to copyright — the phrase brew pub. Is that not so?
That's right.

Is that California, nationally, or worldwide?
I've already gotten California. And I've applied for the federal one. I'd probably then license the use of the word. What's going to happen is, if I hadn't done this, I can assure you that Seagram's or Suntory or some major corporation would've trademarked it.

I'm convinced that you'll be able to go on your bicycle from Seattle, Washington, to San Diego, stopping at brew pub to brew pub. I mean there's going to be that many of 'em within ten years.

You have, I understand, kind of an unusual policy toward customers. Could you explain it?
We have a little sign that says "This Is Not Burger King — You Can't Have It Your Way." In other words, we don't cater to the public.

How do your customers generally feel about that policy?
They love it. They don't bat an eye. I mean if they get up and leave, somebody else sits in their chair.

What would you say is your greatest frustration in the several years you've had the brew pub?
My greatest frustration is getting together the money to build a second one.

What would you say your greatest joy has been?
To have been able to turn a concept into a reality — the brew pub — has been very exciting. And to be one of the pioneers is fun, too.

Bill, thanks very much.
Thank you, Will.

HAYWARD TODAY . . . TOMORROW THE WORLD. Buffalo Bill and his brew pub label (he sells twenty-four ounce bottles of his Buffalo Brew to go). Bill's greatest frustration: trying to round up the three hundred thousand dollars necessary to set up a second place. He's shooting for Marin County but hopes to eventually expand to Los Angeles . . . and maybe even all the way to the East Coast someday.

BUFFALO BILL'S BREW PUB
HAYWARD, CALIFORNIA
BEER
Barley, Hops, Water & Yeast
1 PINT 8 OZ.

Holding a Beer Taste-off

There is no bad beer: some kinds are better than others.
— *Old German proverb*

Old German proverb contain much truth.

A beer that tastes pretty yucky today may taste real fine tomorrow. So much of beer drinking is a reflection of the moment, the mood. The weather, what day of the week it is, what we've just eaten or not eaten, who you're with, whether you've had a fight with your spouse, the freshness of the brew being imbibed, the glass you're using, etc., etc., etc. — all have a significant role in the enjoyment or unenjoyment of a given beer at a given time.

Because of the importance of an individual's moment or mood, I'm not the world's greatest believer in beer-tasting experts or panels. But beer tasting can be fun and can lead to some interesting discoveries . . . the most usual being that a beer you've always considered Old Blemish scores as well as Ye Olde Favorite.

So Hold a Beer Taste-off

It's easy enough to get into some serious beer tasting. Start by selecting an adequate supply of (i.e., plenty of!) eight to ten different brews, making sure there's a range of types. Include an ale or two, some heartier brews, some light, everyday types. Try to ensure all are fresh. Remove the

WITH THINE EYES. Drink to your beer with your eyes first.

labels or otherwise completely disguise each brew, marking each only with its own identifying number or letter. Buy some palate cleaners, too. Saltine crackers and cheese work well.

Next, invite six to ten nectar-of-the-grain buffs over. Give each a rating form . . . and start pouring. Each beer should be served in its own glass (I know . . . ten times ten is a lot of glasses!) and should be appreciated — *slowly* — by itself. Rate each beer for (a) appearance, (b) aroma, (c) taste, and (d) aftertaste. Again, don't just wolf down the beer; savor each characteristic separately and slowly.

Since taste is, of course, the paramount characteristic, I'd use a rating scale of 0 to 4 in judging it, and I'd use a 0-to-2 scale for each of the other three characteristics. In this way a "lovely to look at, lousy to taste" beer will get the low score it deserves.

Cleanse the palate with a cracker and a little cheese. Repeat the pouring and judging for brew number two, and so on.

After all eight or ten brews have been sampled and rated for each characteristic, add up everyone's total scores, eliminate the lowest ranking four or five, and repeat the taste testing using only the top four or five scorers. To build drama — as well as to provide a fine excuse to enjoy more beer — keep on going until you've narrowed the brews down to the best three, the best two, and finally the best one. Kiss it, crown it,

ADEQUATE SUPPLY. Make sure you have an adequate supply of brew.

tie a ribbon around it . . . do something to declare it THE WINNER!

Holding a beer taste-off is a tough job . . . and, done with care and patience, can take several hours. But somebody has to do it. After all, scientific research *is* scientific research!

Appearance: What to Look For

Drink your beer with your eyes before you drink it with your lips. Hold it up to the light. Are the bubbles small? They should be, and they should rise to the top at a slow, relaxed speed. Your beer should have a head that's thick and full bodied. And it should be able to hold it for a while. If the head fades seemingly within seconds of pouring, be wary! You probably have a cheapie on your hands (and in your hand!).

Aroma: What to Smell For

Be sure you've poured the beer right down the middle of the glass to create a full head and to release the brew's full bouquet and aroma. Then go ahead — take a good sniff. It may at first seem strange to be smelling beer. But do it . . . and then do it again.

GO AHEAD. Go ahead . . . take a whiff.

Is the overall experience one of inhaling freshness, cleanliness? Or is it one of inhaling skunkiness? (Try this test with a beer you've had around for quite a while versus the same brand just bought fresh. You'll soon detect the difference between freshness and skunkiness!)

Taste: What to Taste For

Taste buds are very personal things, so what to taste for in a beer is not really for anyone to say. But to get the most out of it — good beer or not so good — try drinking it very slowly. Swish and swill it around in your mouth. Try actually chewing it. Is the beer thick, with a body it can be proud of, or is it thin, like flavored water? Is your beer so highly carbonated that it tastes like it's all bubbles, or does the degree of carbonation taste good against your tongue, in your mouth?

Aftertaste: What to Aftertaste For

Okay, your beer's gone down the hatch, but what memory remains? Is there a bitter taste in your mouth, or is what remains pleasant? Does your mouth feel good? It should.

WHAT REALLY COUNTS. It's the taste that really counts.

AFTERTASTE. Some beers have better aftertaste than others.

Imports: Inching Up

Imported beer — that seemingly endless lineup of brands from far distant lands — makes up but a small percentage of America's total beer sales. That percentage, however, is inching up . . . from 3.9 percent of the total in 1984 to 4.3 percent in 1985.

New York City is far and away the nation's leading metropolitan area in terms of imported beer sales. Big Apple Metro beer drinkers quaffed more than one million barrels of foreign suds in 1984 . . . 14.6 percent of the entire nation's total.

To find out what's hot in the world of imports in the very core of the Apple, *From Beer to Eternity* ventured on down to the East Village to speak with Manny Toreces, proprietor of Toreces' Pantry. Located at Second Avenue and Ninth Street, Toreces' Pantry is one of New York's largest sellers of imported brews.

Manny, you are reputed to be one of the larger sellers of imported beer in New York. Is that true?
Yes, we are. We have one of the largest selections of imported beer in New York. And we're always seeking and trying to locate any new imported beers that are brought in by distributors or importers.

How many brands of imported beer would you say you carry?
Probably close to two hundred. That's a number that's increased over the past few years. Unfortunately, though, some of these products are not what I would call bona fide imports: they're products that've been created for export because of the American demand for imported beers. And consumers are aware enough to pick it up, believe me. They'll try it once because they see the new label, and they'll quickly realize it's an inferior product.

Do you have a lot of people who do that — try a different beer each night or each week?
Lots. Lots. Especially on weekends. They'll come in here and they'll pick out beers for mini tastings. They'll pick a couple of these, a couple of that.

THE PANTRY. Proprietor Manny Toreces flashing his best Second Avenue smile. Although the Pantry doesn't appear very thirst-provoking from the outside, on the inside it's another matter: coolers stocked with close to two hundred imported brews all lined up and ready to go.

What is hot right now?

Well, Belgium beers promoted themselves very well in the beer periodicals and in the press, and they've had a real resurgence of interest. They are selling at a very high price. But some of them, I don't know why people drink them; especially these Lambic beers. I guess they've got some value to their taste, some redeeming cultural value to their taste. But most people say, "Too bitter; the taste is too pronounced." You just can't enjoy it; you have to concentrate on it. It's that kind of beer. It's all consuming. You have to pay attention to what you're drinking.

The Guinness sells well, especially around St. Patrick's Day. The English beers are pricey-er than the other imports; I think people pick 'em up and they'll treat themselves to a Bass when they're drinking one or two, but they won't pick 'em up in quantity. It's a treat for them. Whereas Heineken is probably two dollars less a six-pack . . . people'll pick it up as readily as they'll pick up a Michelob.

What's your own favorite?

It really depends on the mood. Friday afternoon when I'm feeling good I might go for Old Peculiar. Or Anchor Steam. And Panama: it's from Panama. It's a real nice pilsener beer.

But it changes, especially being I'm trying new beers every day. My everyday beer is Rignes, the low-alcohol Rignes . . . that's the one I have at home. It's a lot of flavor for ninety calories.

What trends have you noticed in the past few years?

Lighter: they like lightness in their beer. Even though they swear they love the heavier ales, they'll still consume on a daily basis a lighter beer. Lagers, pilseners, and even leaning towards lighter than the pilsener . . . something with lower caloric content and lower alcohol. Nonalcohol beers are selling very well.

Can you think of any funny or interesting story of someone who came in and bought 28 or so different brands?

No, not 28. We had a guy that bought 130 brands to take them across country. One hundred thirty different. He pulled up in a car. He was living here in the neighborhood, and he was leaving, and he decided to stock up. He just came in and took all his favorites. I guess while he was here he tried a lot of beers!

One hundred thirty favorites: that sounds like a good note on which to end. Thanks, Manny.

It's been a pleasure, Will.

Top 26 Imported Beer Brands
(in millions of gallons)

	1984	1983 (in millions of gallons)	1983–1984 Percent Change	1984 Market Share
1. Heineken	75.60	69.50	9%	33.9%
2. Molson	31.50	29.50	7%	14.1
3. Becks	19.32	16.20	19%	8.7
4. Moosehead	14.40	13.00	11%	6.4
5. Labatt	9.68	9.50	2%	4.3
6. St. Pauli Girl	7.88	5.60	40%	3.5
7. Dos Equis	7.43	6.00	23%	3.3
8. Amstel	4.28	2.50	71%	1.9
9. Guinness	3.80	2.50	52%	1.7
10. Corona	3.77	1.90	102%	1.7
11. Tecate	3.50	3.00	17%	1.6
12. O'Keefe	3.31	3.10	6%	1.5
13. Fosters	2.93	2.70	8%	1.3
14. Kirin	2.28	1.80	26%	1.0
15. Moussy*	2.25	.50	317%	1.0
16. Grizzly	2.25	1.50	50%	1.0
17. Grolsch	2.03	1.90	6%	.9
18. Bass	1.68	1.40	21%	.8
19. Kronenbourg	1.63	1.10	45%	.7
20. Tsingtao	1.62	1.40	17%	.7
21. DAB	1.58	1.20	27%	.7
22. Carta Blanca	1.50	1.20	25%	.7
23. Sapporo	1.42	1.30	11%	.6
24. San Miguel	1.35	1.20	9%	.6
25. Warteck*	1.17	.10	940%	.5
26. Carlsberg	.90	.70	33%	.4
All Others	14.24	15.42	−8%	6.4
Totals	**223.30**	**195.72**	**14.1%**	**100.0%**

*No-alcohol products

THE TOP 26. Nationally it's Heineken by a mile when it comes to imported beer sales. Molson's a distant second, followed by Becks, Moosehead, and Labatt. On Second Avenue and Ninth Street, however, it's a different story. Comments Manny as to how the big sellers line up at his shop: "I see Dos Equis moving up, up there with Molson and Heineken. And Becks's holding its pace. And Amstel much higher. Moosehead was a big seller last year and the year before. It's slowing down quite a bit. Heineken is far and away my biggest seller. Then Molson. And then Becks and Dos Equis tied for third.

Reprinted with permission of *Modern Brewery Age* magazine.

The Joy of Home Brew

As much as I enjoy beer—both in terms of drinking and folklore—I've never been even the least bit tempted to try to make it myself. I guess that's because I know all too well that anything technical or scientific is not at all my forte . . . I'd be apt to blow up half of Brooklyn (I know, "No big loss" most of you are saying). But an awful lot of people DO brew their own beer. To learn more about home brewing and home brewers we spoke with Mr. Home Brew himself, Charlie Papazian of Boulder, Colorado, president of the American Home Brewers Association and author of *The Complete Joy of Home Brewing* (Avon Books).

Charlie, can you try to explain what is the joy of home brewing? Why do people do it?
In this country, by and large, the main reason people are brewing beer for themselves is because of quality. These are people that are home brewing because they enjoy the taste of beer. In other words, what I'm saying is they're not home brew-

ing because of alcohol, that's for sure. It might be different in other countries, but in this country, according to our surveys, people are brewing because they appreciate the taste of beer. They drink a lot of commercially available beer and consequently they get involved with brewing their own and learning more about beer in general—learning how the commercial breweries brew their beer and improving their own.

And the other thing is it's fun. It's a real enjoyable hobby, so to speak, where someone can actually brew a beer and share it with their friends and impress their friends on how good it tastes.

Do you think that most people home brew because they feel they can brew a beer that's better than that which is commercially available?
I would say that most people brew it because they brew a kind of beer they like. I find very few home brewers comparing their beer to commercial beer. It's as good as commercial beer. There are people that say that it's better than commercial beer, but they're in the minority.

But they're not trying to brew something akin to a Budweiser or a Miller, your folks. I would think they were trying to brew something more like Anchor Steam or an IPA or something, aren't they?
I think in general that's true, although there are people that do try to brew a light beer, to lighten up on their recipes to brew a summertime beer that's as quenching as an American pilsener-style beer.

So most people will brew several different types of beer during the year . . . maybe a heavier, heartier ale in the winter and then a lighter beer in the summer?
Yes, exactly. And they'll also have fun with brewing specialty beers, which you very rarely find from commercial brewers. Things like cherry-flavored beer, raspberry-flavored beer. Or they'll even experiment with spice-flavored beers.

Do most people make up their own crazy names and labels?

Yes, a lot of 'em do. We have quite a collection of home brew labels. I can think of things like my own Rocky Raccoon Light Honey Lager.

How many home brewers would you say there are in the country?

There are probably a million people that will home brew this year, 1986. Of these, half of them will be involved enough to brew more than one batch. They're mostly males, aged twenty-five to thirty-five.

Is there a strong predominance geographically?

Yes, there are pockets in the Northeast. There's a pocket in the Northwest. Seattle to Portland. California. A lot of interest here in Colorado. And the midwest, from Wisconsin through Ohio and up into Michigan. That's where we see most of the brewing.

Would you say that home brewing is growing at a rapid rate?

It's been stable for the last year and a half. It grew tremendously in 1979, when it was legalized. And when it became legalized, the quality of the products — as far as home brewing ingredients and equipment — not only proliferated, but the quality went way up. And also good information became available to home brewers . . . techniques that enabled a first-time brewer to be able to brew a beer — simply — that would no doubt in my mind be comparable to something that one would pay five dollars to six dollars a six-pack for in an imported section of a liquor store.

What are the costs involved in home brewing?

It costs one dollar a six-pack for home brew, for a beer that a lot of people would call in this country super premium or import quality. And it only costs about thirty dollars for the equipment needed to get started.

Fun, tasty, economical . . . sounds like a good deal. Thanks for sharing the joy of home brewing with us, Charlie.

Thank you, Will.

WONDERFUL AND/OR WACKY. If one-third of the fun of home brew is brewing it and a second third is drinking it . . . then a third third must be in making up wonderful and/or wacky labels. Here are a few from the collection of the American Homebrewers Association, including Charlie's own Blitzweizen Barley Wine Lager ("A Barley Wine before its time is like a mountain without a peak").

What's on Tap?

North & Eisner's Bar, Baltimore, circa 1935 (Photo courtesy *Baltimore News-American*)

Call it draught...

Call it draft...

Call it tap...

...but call it good!

Call it draught ... call it draft ... call it tap. There's nothing quite like a pitcher or mug or glass of beer right out of the barrel. For awhile, though, it looked as if the time might come when you could get the pitcher or mug or glass but not the beer. Draft sales — as a percentage of total U.S. beer sales — declined steadily every year from 1934 until 1979, when they staged a most welcome comeback. Since then draft has been inching up as a percentage of America's total beer sales, though it's a far cry from "the good old days."

To get the lowdown on just what is different about draft beer — and what makes it taste so good — I spoke with one of the nation's more outspoken draft beer advocates, Mr. New Jersey Draft Beer of 1986 (and most likely 1987, too!), Augie Helms, of Union, New Jersey.

"Augie, just what is the difference between draft beer and packaged beer?"
Well, as we all know, it's a matter of, for one thing, storage life. There are chemicals added to the packaged beer. There's shelf life chemicals.

And packaged beer is gassier, too. It has higher carbonation. It's a false carbonation. The carbonation is introduced into the bottle for shelf life. When you pour yourself a

"Juke joint," south central Florida, February 1941 (Photo courtesy Library of Congress)

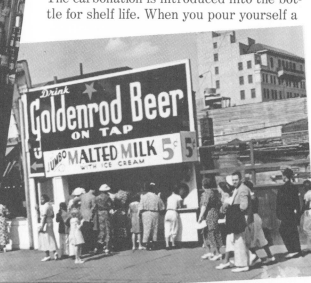

Beverage stand, Coney Island, New York, July 4, 1936 (Photo courtesy U.S. History, Local History & Genealogy Division, The New York Public Library, Astor, Lenox and Tilden Foundations)

bottle of beer, you kick up quite a head. Try this test yourself: pour yourself a draft beer, holding the glass way down as you pour it. And then do the same with a bottle at the same height, and you'll see the gas kickup from the bottle is enormous.

And, of course, packaged beer is pasteurized. In other words, they have a product and they're tampering with it by reboiling it, in essence. They say there's no consistency with bottled beer because of this pasteurization process, whereas the draft beer is not pasteurized and it's pretty consistent. I mean, why tamper with a product that's been doing pretty good?

What makes draft beer taste so good? Well, the high carbonation of packaged beers gives you a bite on the tongue, which I think deadens your taste buds. It's like champagne; it's a bubbly effect. It's not the true end of the brewmaster's art, whereas keg beer is. That's the way beer was meant to be . . . served in kegs.

Draft Beer Sales as a % of Total United States Beer Sales	
Year	%
1934	74.8
1935	70.5
1940	48.4
1945	35.6
1950	28.2
1955	22.1
1960	19.3
1965	17.7
1970	14.1
1975	12.4
1980	12.1
1985	13.1

Source: U.S. Brewers Association

TWO-FISTED. Augie Helms, a two-fisted beer drinker doing what he likes to do best . . . drinking draft beer.

Augie sums up most bottled beer in one word—"insipid." As for canned beer, Mr. New Jersey Draft Beer of 1986 swears he can often almost taste the metal from the can. What it all boils down to for Augie is: if it isn't draft, you can pretty much forget it.

Bartender, San Diego, circa 1940. (Photo courtesy San Diego Historical Society—Ticor Collection)

GONE ARE THE DAYS. They don't make valentines as clever as this anymore.

JUST A BIG MUG

WHO'D LIKE TO "DRAUGHT" YOU FOR HIS VALENTINE

Continued on next page

A BARREL OF LAUGHS. You're not likely to split your sides over this circa 1950 postcard beer humor. But, then again, you probably don't much care to split your sides anyway: it might interfere with your enjoyment of the rest of *From Beer to Eternity*...and that would never do!

Beer Seer

He's been gone for half a century now, but his memory still lurks in the haunts and hearts of Chicago: the beer seer, Kharma the Mystic.

With Kharma you could keep your palms in your pockets, your tea leaves at home; what he wanted was to get at your beer foam. Not your beer. You drank that...then Kharma would dive, figuratively speaking, into the glass and read your future by the tracings of foam left around the sides. What would appear to anyone else as just plain old foam became much more to Kharma's trained eye and fertile mind: it became the key to the future.

Not any old beer gave the best results, though. The beer seer liked to work with rich, creamy foam, which, of course, meant that he liked his subjects to drink rich, creamy beer. Beers with thin, scanty foam left few tracings with which to pursue the intriguing art of divination.

Hired by Chicago's Birk Brothers Brewing Co. to promote their Superb Beer—which just happened to have a rich, creamy head—Kharma translated the mysteries of the foam into the mysteries of the future for many, many a Chicagoland beer quaffer in the late 1930s. Some say the town's never been the same since.

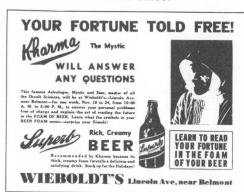

A 1937 newspaper ad heralding Kharma the Mystic.

Doing It with Vitamins

There's always been barley and hops and water. There's often been corn or rice. And for a time in the late 1930s, there were vitamins.

Schlitz announced the addition of vitamin D to its beer in early 1936. In ads in major markets across the country, the Milwaukee giant hailed it as "one of the greatest brewing achievements of all time!"

In early 1937 the Auto City Brewing Co., of Detroit went Schlitz one vitamin better. It started putting vitamins B and G (riboflavin) in its Altweiser Beer. Ad copy stressed that now Altweiser "is more refreshing because of the vitamins B and G which it contains. These are the vitamins which are absolutely essential to proper digestion."

What next? Well what was next was the Federal Alcoholic Administration's (FAA) ruling in early 1940 that beer labeling could not make mention of vitamins. The FAA's reasoning: such labeling might lead some consumers to believe that beer had curative value.

ONE THING'S FOR SURE. Regardless of rules or regulations or bans, you can always play it safe, as this Minnesota bar did, and claim...(turn upside down)

The Beer That Made Milwaukee Famous

The Refreshing Part of Every Party

JOS. SCHLITZ BREWING CO. Milwaukee, Wis.

An ad from 1937 for Schlitz, the Sunshine Vitamin Beer.

"There are two reasons for drinking . . . when you are thirsty, to cure it; the other, when you are not thirsty, to prevent it."

— *Thomas L. Peacock*

On the Importance of the Bottle Cap

OUT WITH THE OLD. The lightning stopper was the most successful bottle-stopping device tried before William Painter's crown top arrived on the scene.

IN WITH THE NEW. The crown cap: fit for a king... and millions upon millions of bottles since 1891.

Be it ever so humble, the bottle cap is no big deal... but that's because it works. If it didn't, it would be a big deal. Your beer would be flat and/or brimming with all kinds of dirt and other floating goodies.

Until 1891 how to properly seal a bottle *was* a big deal. In the forty years between 1850 and 1890, well over a thousand different bottle-stopping devices were considered by brewers and bottlers. None of them, however, really did the job. Dirt all too often got in and carbonation all too often got out.

Just when it appeared as though lovers of bottled beer might forever be crying in flat beer... Shazam! In stepped the hero of the day, a gentleman from Baltimore named William Painter. Painter had an uncanny knack for solving mechanical problems. His various and diverse inventions earned him the hefty total of eighty-five patents dur-

ing his lifetime. None, however, was more important than the one he perfected while on vacation in 1891, the crown top.

What made Painter's top, still in use today, so revolutionary was that it was really a cover rather than a stopper. The name *crown* comes from the top's striking resemblance to a king's crown.

Although not all brewers jumped aboard the crown top bandwagon in the years immediately following 1891, quite a few did; and with each succeeding year, it became ever more obvious than the crown top would eventually be the only top.

So...

So the next time you open a bottle of beer, maybe you shouldn't just toss the cap away. You might want to look at it, admire it, appreciate it — maybe even frame it.

Champagne Music for the Champagne of Beer

In 1903, Milwaukee's Fred. Miller Brewing Co. sponsored a contest to come up with a slogan for their brand new High Life bottled beer. The winner was "The Champagne of Bottled Beer."

Forty-six years later, in 1949, the brewery signed up Mr. Champagne Music himself, Lawrence Welk, to sing and orchestrate the praises of High Life on Welk's weekly radio show. Shown here, inking the contract, are Welk, Miller advertising manager Roy J. Bernier, and the Champagne Man's vocalist, Helen Ramsey.

ON THE DOTTED LINE. But did they celebrate with champagne or beer?!

Malt Liquor: It's Got That Extra Zing

Pop a malt liquor and you're popping powerful stuff. It tastes like beer, though more bitter, but it's got an alcohol percentage that's mucho higher. The alcohol content in regular beer ranges from 3 percent to 5 percent; for malt liquor it starts at 5 percent and can go as high as 9 percent.

Malt liquor is predominantly a male province, especially an urban male province. In total it accounts for but 4 percent or so of the overall U.S. beer market.

GLIX. Malt liquor's been around longer than most people realize. Here's a Glix Malt Liquor label that's working on being fifty years old. It dates from 1939. Glix Malt Liquor was brewed by the Grand Valley Brewing Co. of Ionia, Michigan, in the late thirties and early forties. It was also later brewed from 1958 through 1965 by the Glueck Brewing Co. of Minneapolis.

"IT WORKS EVERY TIME." The message is macho—and not a little suggestive, too—in this 1986 ad for Colt 45. In addition to Colt 45 (G. Heileman), other mainstays in the malt liquor market include Champale (Iroquois Brands), Olde English "800" (Pabst), King Cobra (Anheuser-Busch), Haffenreffer Private Stock (Falstaff), Magnum (Miller), Schlitz Malt Liquor (Stroh), and Mickey's (G. Heileman).

Schmidting Pretty

To celebrate their one hundred thirtieth birthday in December 1985, the folks at St. Paul, Minnesota's Schmidt Brewery decided to hold a "family reunion" par excellence. They invited every Schmidt in Twin Citiesland to come on down to the brewery on the big day, December 17, to join in the birthday festivities and enjoy a brew or two.

Becoming a Schmidt for a day and joining in the birthday blast were St. Paul mayor George Latimer and Minnesota governor Rudy Perpich. The highlight of the day: when 130 radio stations throughout the entire North Star State played Happy Birthday at 5:30 P.M.

SCHMIDT'S A HIT. Over 1,500 Schmidts were invited to share some of their namesake brew. Here's a bunch who're doing just that. (Photo courtesy G. Heileman Brewing Co.)

I See the Light, I See the Lite

The word *light* has foamed its way through an intriguing—one could even say confusing—evolution in America's brewing history. Until Prohibition, light generally meant the opposite of dark: there were dark—as in brunette—beers; and there were light—as in blond—beers. Sometimes there were even medium—as in dirty blond—beers.

But in the thirties, forties, and fifties, the word *light* came to generally mean the opposite of heavy . . . brews with less body, brews that were, to be honest, more watery tasting. In fact there are those who say that the real impetus to lightness was provided during World War II by the at-home army of "Rosie the Riveter" female war workers. Exposed to considerable beer drinking for the first time, "Rosie" would literally cut her beer with water. Brewers, pressed with stringent wartime grain quotas as it was, got the message and began to brew it that way, with less barley malt, more corn and/or rice.

By the late sixties and especially the early seventies, the word was evolving one more time . . . to mean less calories. In its new usage, the word is often spelled —actually misspelled—as *Lite*.

Today, not surprisingly, *light* is a confusing word when it comes to beer. Bud Light is a low-calorie beer, although Piel's Light is not. And there are still light beers as

contrasted to the Prior Double Darks and the Beck Darks of the world.

Buying a light beer is . . . enlightening.

Tripping the Lite Fantastic

In 1972 Miller acquired the rights to the name's and formulas of the Meister Brau Brewing Co. of Chicago. One of those formulas was for Lite Beer, a brand Meister Brau had been marketing in the midwest since May 1967. Actually the basic formula for Lite had been developed by the Buckeye Brewing Co. of Toledo, a firm that Meister Brau had itself absorbed in 1966.

Meister Brau had at best mixed success with Lite, but with Miller it has been a completely different story. They improved the formula and started pumping money into advertising and promoting it:

$　　400,000 in 1973
$　4,000,000 in 1974
$10,000,000 in 1975
$12,000,000 in 1976

Money talks, but Miller also developed some of the catchiest commercials ever to come down the beer pike . . . and people listened —and bought.

They're still listening. And they're still buying. It's safe to say that if it hadn't been for Miller's whole-hog decision with Lite, there'd be no Light/Lite market today. They created the market, and in spite of a seeming army of other Lights, they still dominate the market.

And that's no Lite feat!

LESS FILLING. Sorry John Madden, Rodney Dangerfield, Whitey Ford, Bubba Smith, and all you other Miller Lite spokesmen, but Ruppert's Knickerbocker beat you to the punch with "Less Filling" way back in the mid-fifties. And Knickerbocker wasn't even a low-calorie beer.

FIRST IN SALES IN MASSACHUSETTS!

Ask the boy for the "Less Filling Beer!"

Knickerbocker
New York's Famous Beer

RUPPERT KNICKERBOCKER BEER, JACOB RUPPERT, N. Y. C.

96

A great tasting beer—A light beer with less calories than skim milk

99 CALORIES

GABLINGER'S BEER

12 Fl. Oz.
Forest Brewing Co., New Bedford, Mass.

YOUR GROCER HAS IT

LESS CALORIES THAN SKIM MILK. A 1974 newspaper ad for Gablinger's. Its slogan was "Grab a Gab." Few beer drinkers did.

"Uncle Billy" Smulowitz

JUST WHAT IS LIGHT/LITE BEER, ANYWAY? Well, Bill Smulowitz, president of Wilkes-Barre's The Lion, Inc., brewers of Steg (Stegmaier) Light, explains it this way: "Basically light beer has a lower content of calories and carbohydrates. These elements are reduced through longer and more complete fermentation. There are numerous processes to achieve the end result. In the final analysis, it's all accomplished in the brewhouse by the brewmaster."

OTTO HUBER BREWERY

Golden Rod Beer.

LIGHT, - - -	$1.20	per case of 24 bottles.
MEDIUM (Standard) -	1.10	
DARK (Muenchner) -	1.25	

ORDER FROM YOUR GROCER, OR DIRECT.

Telephone, 1883 W'msburg, Borough of Brooklyn.
" 2902, 38th St., " " Manhattan.

O. H. Extract of Malt, $2 per case of one dozen bottles.

LIGHT, MEDIUM, DARK. An announcement from Brooklyn's Otto Huber Brewery from the September 9, 1901, program of the Madison Square Garden Theatre, New York City. At that time Madison Square Garden really was located on Madison Square, at Madison Avenue and Twenty-seventh Street.

Why the Medium is the least expensive is unknown . . . but at those prices who'd care anyway?

THE GOOD DOCTOR'S BEER. One of the very earliest of light —meaning low-calorie—beers didn't even use the word *light* on its label. But, then again, Gablinger's had so many problems it wasn't sure if it was coming or going anyway.

Introduced by Rheingold in 1967, Gablinger's immediately ran afoul of government red tape. The Food and Drug Administration said that because Gablinger's was marketed for "Special Dietary Use," the label had to state the number of calories contained. The Federal Alcoholic Administration Act, however, prohibited alcoholic beverage ads that mentioned calories.

Caught in the middle, Rheingold was in and out of court for two years before the government made up its mind and allowed the number of calories to be put on Gablinger's label. During the two-year period, Gab sales went nowhere. But it wasn't just government bureaucracy that held sales back. Gablinger's was packaged in an *ugly* brown can and featured a picture of Dr. Gablinger—the good Swiss doctor who'd invented it—without ever saying who he was . . . or what he was doing on your can of beer.

Ropkins' Light Dinner Ale

Seventy per cent. Malt. Thirty per cent. Cereal. Hops to flavor, no sugar, no glucose. Our ale is absolutely pure. Government Serial No. 45127. See that the ALE you drink is as pure as this. Measure the contents of our bottle with the ordinary bottle. 'Phone your dealer or direct.

Ropkins & Company
Hartford   Telephone Charter 4034

LIGHT DINNER ALE. Before Prohibition most American brewers produced ale as well as lager. Many brewed both a dark ale, à la porter, and a light ale. Here's a rather smart ad for Light Dinner Ale from Hartford, Connecticut's Ropkins & Company.

Continued on next page

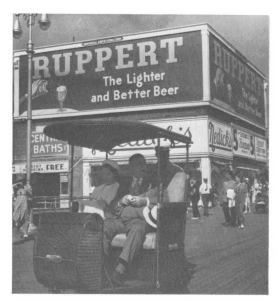

Coney Island, New York, July 1939 (Photo courtesy Museum of the City of New York)

Piel's Light

Prior to Prohibition Brooklyn's Piel Bros. brewed Piel's Real German Lager Beer, a hearty brew they promoted — especially when beer shipments were cut off from Europe during World War I — as being equal to imported. After Prohibition, however, they made the switch to light lager in a big way and have stayed with it, through several changes in ownership, ever since. Piel's Light Beer is still on many a supermarket and package store shelf throughout the East . . . but it means light as in not heavy, as opposed to light as in low calorie.

DE-LIGHT-FUL. A hodgepodge of Piel's Light pieces, including their first beer can design, from 1938, and their most recent. The "Light" is still there.

Lighter, Lighter, Lighter

For more than fifty years now, the trend at most American breweries has been lighter, lighter, lighter. Some beer quaffers would more likely call it blander, blander, blander. Their view: if you want to drink water, get yourself a glassful out of the tap; if you want to drink beer, pour yourself something with some body, some character, some heart.

Rainier Beer billboard, Seattle, Washington, circa 1965 (Photo courtesy Foster and Kleiser)

MR. TOUGH GUY. Sometimes it takes a tough brewmaster to make a tender beer.

Do Your Part, Buy the Quart

How'd you like to be a hero by buying beer by the quart? And drinking it by the quart, too?

Sound a little too good to be true?

Well, it was true back in World War II. Metal, vital to the war effort, was in short supply. Beer cans had already been prohibited for use on the home front. Now it was time to ration bottle caps, made largely of tin. Buying quarts instead of the usual twelve-ounce bottle meant that the consumer allowed one cap to do the work of almost three.

As explained by New York's Jacob Ruppert Brewery in a large, October 1942, *New York Times* ad:

> CAPS OFF TO UNCLE SAM. Every time you buy mellow light Ruppert in the big "Victory" Quart Size you save vital war metal. And you get 32 grand-tasting ounces of mellow light beer, enough to fill four big glasses, for less money. And, it's easier to carry — easier to store in your icebox — easier to serve. BUY THE RUPPERT "VICTORY" QUART.

Baltimore's Gunther Brewing Co. was considerably more poetic — and dramatic — about it:

> Sound the bugle, roll the drum,
>   And let the cannon roar!
> Give a cheer, lads, here they come . . .
>   The Pride of Baltimore!
> To blast the Germans and the Japs,
>   On many a distant shore.
> The little Gunther bottle caps
>   Are marching off to war!

It's Now the 1980s
There aren't too many bottle caps marching off to war nowadays. Does it still make sense to buy beer by the quart? You bet it does.

> Times may have changed,
> World War II is over . . .
> But if you buy beer by the quart
> You'll still be in the clover.
>   . . . actually the hops.
> And, if you save the caps . . . you'll be the tops!

HELP TO WIN — SAVE THE TIN. Beer ads from 1942, the year the War Production Board began the rationing of bottle caps . . . and we had Victory Quarts as well as Victory Gardens.

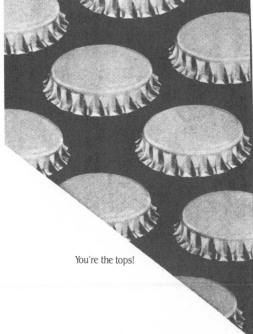

You're the tops!

Pride of Newark

ALE, ALE, THE GANG'S ALL HERE. Feigenspan put out a full range of malt beverages under the P.O.N. name. Two P.O.N. Ale cans: the one on the left dates from the early 1940s, the one on the right from the late 1930s.

Pride in Newark, the city that Rand McNally's 1985 *Places Rated Almanac* ranked among the bottom 3 percent of America's metropolitan areas with respect to housing and the worst 11 percent with respect to crime.

You have to be kidding!

But there is pride in Newark. The same Newark that scored so abysmally in housing and crime scored in the top 6 percent with respect to the arts, education, and health care/environment . . . right up there with the nation's best.

Newark's beer output has traditionally ranked with the nation's best, too. Names such as P. Ballantine & Sons, Hensler, Krueger, and Hoffman come readily to the mind of brewery and beer buffs. Pabst brewed in Newark from 1946 until 1985. And it was in Newark that Anheuser-Busch constructed its first plant outside of St. Louis. Opened in 1951, it's a plant that has brewed and continues to brew a lot of Bud and Michelob for the East Coast market.

But the brewery that probably most personified Newark's brewing heritage was the Christian Feigenspan Brewing Company, brewer of P.O.N. — Pride of Newark.

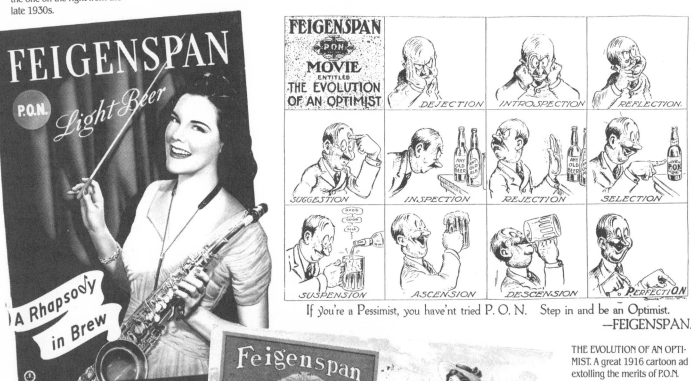

A RHAPSODY IN BREW. An early 1940s sign proclaiming P.O.N. Light Beer to be "A Rhapsody in Brew," a slogan coined by the brewery in 1940. *Modern Brewery Age,* the leading trade journal of the day, heralded it as "one of the catchiest phrases ever used in beer advertising."

THE EVOLUTION OF AN OPTIMIST. A great 1916 cartoon ad extolling the merits of P.O.N.

MANY SPRINGS AGO. Here's a 1913 postcard announcing the arrival of bock season.

100

Near Beer: Beer That Really Isn't Beer

The man who called it "near beer" was a bad judge of distance.
— attributed to both Philander Johnson in *Shooting Stars* and to Luke McLuke, columnist for the *Cincinnati Enquirer*.

There has been an abundance of nonalcoholic brews to hit the American market in the last several years. Fueled by tough drinking and driving laws, the brews include such longtime American standbys as Kingsbury, Goetz, and Zing, plus a seemingly endless supply of imports. Many of the imports, lead by Moussy, have come pouring out of Switzerland. Since the early 1970s, the sale of alcoholic beverages has been prohibited in restaurants along Switzerland's highways, and Swiss brewers have been working hard to develop palatable near beers. To qualify as a near beer, the brew must contain less than 0.5 percent alcohol. Contrary to the above quote from Prohibition days, quite a few of today's near beers aren't really that bad at all, and that includes our own American brews, as well as the more expensive Swiss, German, etc. entries. Try them alone; or mixed half and half with regular beer, they let you enjoy a six-pack . . . with the alcohol intake of a three-pack. Not a bad idea at times.

UREEKA! Near beers — and even near ales — abounded before and during Prohibition. Here are a few that experienced some degree of popularity in the 1915-1933 period.

GET YOUR NEAR BEER HERE. A lineup of some of today's non-alcoholic brews. From the United States: Kingsbury (G. Heileman, LaCrosse, Wisconsin); Metbrau (Metropolis, Trenton, New Jersey); Texas Light (Pearl, San Antonio); Steinbrau (Eastern, Hammonton, New Jersey). From Switzerland: Moussy; Elan; Warteck; Alpenstein. And back to the United States again for that great contradiction in terms: Texas Light Dark (also from Pearl, San Antonio).

From Cars to Carling's

ALL THAT THE NAME IMPLIES. A 1916 and a circa 1930 ad for Peerless. The company's slogan "All that the name implies," was rooted in validity. In 1900, its first year in the auto business, Peerless introduced its "White Streak" model at New York City's Madison Square Automobile Show (the very first auto show held in America, incidentally). Next came the company's "Green Dragon." With famed driver Barney Oldfield at the wheel, the then zero-to-fifty-mile-per-hour record was set in 1904 in a "Green Dragon." The following year Oldfield set the world's first thousand-mile nonstop run with a Peerless at Brighton Beach, New York. By 1931 Peerless was the only exhibitor from the 1900 Auto Show still in business... a tribute to its automotive craftsmanship.

Just as breweries were converted to some unusual uses during Prohibition, so were a host of seemingly most unbrewery-like buildings converted into breweries after Prohibition. The most intriguing of these "How are you ever going to make a brewery out of that?!" conversions involved a long-standing and respected automobile manufacturer.

As of 1932, the Peerless Motor Car Corporation, located on Quincy Avenue in Cleveland, had been producing quality autos for thirty-two years. The problem was that they were producing low- and medium-priced quality autos ... and so were running smack-dab up against the big three: Ford, General Motors, and Chrysler. Besides, depression days were dogging America and cars were not selling well for anyone, regardless of price. Peerless president James A. Bohannon felt strongly that the time was right to get out of cars and into something else. And nothing else looked better than beer. Peerless stockholders agreed.

Enter Carling's. As explained by Bohannon:

It was a long jump from motors to malt and hub caps to hops, but when our directors decided to convert the plant of Peerless Motor Car Corporation into the most modern brewery in America, I found many of the same principles applied. Having lived in Detroit, right across the river from Canada, I always had a proper respect for Carling's. On a quality basis I associated it with Cadillac, Steinway, and Tiffany. So when at Peerless we had a chance to acquire the American rights, formulas, and technical assistance of Canadian Breweries, Ltd., brewers of Carling's Ale, we were quick to take advantage of it. We had a big, modern plant and lots of ambition, and they had the name. It was a natural.

It was a gutsy decision, but a good one. Early in the fall of 1933 the remodeling of the huge plant was begun. Interiors and exteriors of most of the twenty-one–acre complex were reconstructed to allow for the most efficient layout possible. And because there was no obsolete brewing equipment to worry about, the most modern machinery money could buy was soon in place. Brewing operations began in March 1934, and three months later, on June 15, the newly named Brewing Corporation of America threw wide its doors for a giant open house. Over twenty thousand visitors had a fine time enjoying the former automobile manufacturer's first brew, Carling's Red Cap Ale.

Red Cap was quickly followed by Carling's Amber Creme Ale, a slightly lighter ale brewed only until 1938. A third brew, Carling's Black Label Lager Beer, "with a color of golden yellow and a flavor of smooth tartness," was introduced to Americans in December 1934. The Brewing Corporation of America was off and running!

It was to be a good run. Within two decades, in 1953, the brewery topped the coveted "one million barrels sold in a year" mark. In January of the next year, the company name was changed to Carling Brewery Co.

In the 1970s, however, Carling and its Cleveland brewery went their separate ways. In 1971 Carling sold the plant to Philadelphia brewer C. Schmidt & Sons, moving operations to other plants. Then in 1979, Carling was acquired by G. Heileman, a LaCrosse, Wisconsin, brewer making a major move in the game of big brewery musical chairs. By that time Carling (which had become Carling National through some moves of its own) was consistently among America's top dozen brewers ... not bad for a company that started the century with nary a thought of malt or hops, or beer or ale.

LUCY AND ARTHUR AND CARLING'S. Celebrities Arthur Fiedler and Lucille Ball touting the merits of Red Cap Ale in the early 1950s. At the time, Ms. Ball was the star of a radio show entitled "My Favorite Husband," which was soon to make the move to television ... and become the basis for the classic "I Love Lucy."

Today both Red Cap Ale and Black Label are marketed by Heileman as "price" beers ... meaning a lot of beer for the buck.

ARCHITECTURALLY OUTSTANDING. The automobile-plant-turned-brewery as it appeared in a 1938 artist's sketch. Described as recently as 1982 as "architecturally outstanding" by George Hilton, editor of the National Association of Breweriana Advertising's quarterly magazine, *The Breweriana Collector,* it was operated by C. Schmidt & Sons as its midwestern arm until late 1984. It is now idle.

Will the Real Rheingold Please Stand Up?

There's but one Rheingold brewed in America today ... and even that's brewed in Philadelphia, leaps and bounds away from its birthplace in Brooklyn. As with Budweiser, however, there used to be a bunch of them, Rheingolds, that is, and a fair number of claims as to which was the first and/or the "real" one.

The major contenders were:

S. Liebmann's Sons Brewing Co. of Brooklyn, which started marketing a beer they called Rheingold in 1889

The United States Brewing Co. of Chicago, which first used the name Rheingold for their beer on January 1, 1890

The Weisbrod & Hess Brewing Co. of Philadelphia, which registered Rheingold as a trademarked name in 1898

Weisbrod & Hess filed a petition with the Pennsylvania Secretary of State in 1933 in an attempt to void Liebmann's use of Rheingold as a brand name. They lost but continued to brew their Rheingold until they went out of business in the late 1930s. That left the United States Brewing Co. and S. Liebmann's Sons. The United States Brewing Co. brewed its Rheingold until it, too, went out of business in 1955. That left S. Liebmann's Sons, and its Rheingold — or a descendant of its Rheingold — is still with us today.

But there were other, more lightweight, contenders. The Yakima Brewing and Bottling Co. of Yakima, Washington, brewed a brand they called Rheingold from 1934 to 1938. The Voight Brewery Co. of Detroit sold Voight's Rheingold throughout Michigan and neighboring states prior to Prohibition. Then there were assorted Rhein Kings, Rheinbraus, Rhein-Braus, and Rheinlanders. The fascination with the word *rhein* is easily explained: Rhein is the German word for Rhine. Actually it might better be said that Rhine is the English word for Rhein. After all, it is their river.

Das Rheingold

Wagner's classic opera *Das Rheingold* was the inspiration for at least two Rheingolds and, probably directly or indirectly, for all of them. How the United States Brewing Co.'s Rheingold came to be was told on the back of their can, as pictured here, in and around 1950.

The Brooklyn-born Liebmann was likewise the result of Wagner's work. David Liebmann, grandson of brewery founder Samuel Liebmann, loved his opera. After the season of 1889, which had seemed especially satisfying to David, he hosted a bash for Anton Seidl, head of the Met and a close friend of David's, and the entire opera company.

To enliven things, David had the brewery create a special brew, and because the last performance of the season had been *Das Rheingold*, he instructed that the special brew be light and gold ... and he named it Rheingold.

The story would have ended right here, except that the brew turned out to be a smash success ... such a smash success that David convinced the powers that be at the brewery that Rheingold should be added to the firm's product line. It was, and it went over with the public as well as it had at the opera party, becoming Liebmann's top seller within the space of but a few years. Das Rheingold ... Das Good!

Approaching One Hundred

Standing tall — and the only Rheingold still standing at all — is Liebmann's former Rheingold, now brewed by C. Schmidt & Sons, of Philadelphia. When Liebmann (renamed Rheingold Breweries in 1964) shut down in 1976, Schmidt's bought the rights to the name, and they've been brewing Rheingold ever since. One hopes that, along with their brewing, they're getting ready for one heck of a birthday blast, for 1989 marks one hundred years since Rheingold first started quenching thirsts in and around the Big Apple.

AND A RHINEGOLD, TOO. Here's a small lineup of Rheingoldiana, plus a circa 1895 bottle that once held Bowler's Rhinegold Lager. Harry F. Bowler was an Amsterdam, New York, brewer from 1889 until his death in 1916. His estate then carried on until 1920, when Prohibition put an end to Rhinegold, just as it did to so many other American beers.

Pasteur: Doing His Thing for France

LOUIS PASTEUR. Noted French scientist and the father of pasteurization.

Pasteur = Pasteurization = Milk. Right?

Wrong.

Louis Pasteur was most definitely not working with milk when he discovered the process that today bears his name. Nope, he was a good Frenchman working with beer, a good Frenchman determined to figure out a way to make French beer better than German beer, and to thus at least partially avenge France's terrible trouncing at the hands of the Germans in the Franco-Prussian War.

Pasteur's findings, published in 1876 under the title *Études Sur La Bière* (*Studies on Beer*), included the discovery that flash heating killed the bacteria that so readily caused spoilage in beer. The discovery was to prove a major breakthrough for the world's brewers. No longer would beer go bad within days or weeks of its being bottled. The only problem, from Pasteur's point of emotion, was that Germany was part of the world. His discovery helped the brewers of Germany every bit as much as it did those in his beloved France.

C'est très misérable!

Long Before There Was Budweiser

Herodotus, famous Greek historian, wrote a treatise on beer in 460 B.C.

Well before the Spanish arrived in the New World, the Incas of South America enjoyed a beer they made from corn.

Julius Caesar was known to hoist many a flagon of good Roman brew in his day. When his troops pulled off their famous crossing of the Rubicon, you can be sure he didn't toast them with seltzer. No sir, it was beer all around for his boys... and for himself, too.

106

Long before there was Budweiser or Miller or Coors — or even Yuengling — there was beer.

In Mesopotamia, archaeologists have found pieces of pottery that clearly prove that there was brewing going on almost eight thousand years ago. And that ancient land's Queen Shu-Bad is known to have added a touch of class — and a lot of bubbles, too — to her beer by sipping it through a golden straw.

In Babylon, priests knew how to make — and did make — over fifteen different varieties of beer more than four thousand years before the birth of Christ. Included in the varieties were dark beer, pale beer, red beer, three-fold beer, beer with a head, and beer without a head, among others.

The ancient Egyptians placed great importance on the proper brewing of beer. It was, in fact, held in an almost mythical sense, a gift from Ibis, the goddess of nature. Nevertheless, a high government official was appointed the equivalent of Superintendent of Breweries and was charged with ensuring that the "gift" turned out just right.

The Egyptians called their beer *hek* and made it by crumbling chunks of barley bread into jars, filling them with water, and allowing the resultant mixture to ferment. For those unpleasant trips across the desert, only the fermented bread crumbs were brought along. When an oasis was reached, water was added and, voilà, the result was instant beer.

Beer was very much the beverage of the Egyptian upper crust. They served it in gold-inlaid goblets and drank to the toast: "Here's beer for your ghost!" And when Queen Tiy, wife of Amenhotep III (1,375 B.C.) wanted to impress the royal social circle, she'd host a gala that featured duck, gazelle, and porcupine, all washed down with plenty of brew.

The Egyptians knew the health value of beer, too. Pharmacists of the day relied on a list of seven hundred prescriptions, one hundred of which contained beer.

An Assyrian tablet thought to date from 2,000 B.C. proves anew that Noah knew a good thing when he saw it: beer was listed as one of the items he took aboard his ark.

The Greeks, too, liked their brew. Famed playwright Sophocles had a diet he touted for moderation. Its mainstays were bread, meat, plenty of vegetables, and, of course, beer.

With the passing of the Babylonian and Egyptian empires, the Hebrews came to the rescue. In the early days of Christianity, it was the Jewish people who best carried on the art of brewing, introducing it to many other cultures in the process. Beer is mentioned frequently in the Talmud, and at least three of the rabbis who compiled it were themselves brewers.

Think of Vikings and you're apt to think of their gregarious appetites with respect to many of life's pleasures. Beer was no exception. They regularly ate six meals a day . . . and at all six, a soup made of bread and beer was included. They believed that the spirit of a fallen warrior went straight to Valhalla, a humongous banquet hall where thirsts were quenched with tremendous quantities of beer.

Even the Chinese and the Indians got in the act. The Chinese developed a cereal beverage well before the coming of Christ, and the Incas brewed beer from maize (corn) at least several hundred years before the Spanish arrived on the scene.

Long before there was Budweiser . . .

Beer made from wheat was a favorite of the ancient Romans and Gauls.

On the Raging–and Ever-engaging–Question of Beer and Skittles

Beer: *a malted and hopped somewhat bitter alcoholic beverage.*
Skittles: *English ninepines played by pitching or sliding a wooden disk or rolling a wooden ball to knock down pins.*
Beer and Skittles: *drink and play; easygoing enjoyment.*

> — *Webster's Third New International Dictionary*

They don't mind it: it's a regular holiday to them—all porter and skittles.

> — Charles Dickens,
> *Pickwick Papers*, 1836–37

Life isn't all beer and skittles; but beer and skittles, or something better of the same sort, must form a good part of every Englishman's education.

> — Thomas Hughes,
> *Tom Brown's Schooldays*, 1857

Life is with such all beer and skittles;
They are not difficult to please
About their vituals.

> — Charles Stuart Calverley,
> *Contentment*, circa 1880

Life ain't all beer and skittles, and more's the pity.

> — George DuMaurier, *Trilby*, 1891

Beer and skittles . . . that's the thing,
Beer and skittles . . . it's a
   real happening.
They go so well together, without
   a doubt
Nine pins, and porter, ale or stout.
But truth be known, if push should
   come to shove,
Skip the skittles . . . it's the beer
   I really love.

> — Will Anderson, 1986

When Beer Cans Came with "How to Open" Instructions

Yes

KRUEGER BEER *in* CANS *now*

•

Popping a can of beer is about the easiest thing there is to do, but it wasn't always so. There was a time, back in the can's beginnings in the mid and late thirties, when you had to work to get the beer out of the can. Well, not really work, but at least put some effort into it. First of all, the early beer can was built like a brick brewhouse ... solid and tough and at least partially openproof. Those were the days when it really did take a man (or one heck of a strong woman) to crush a can. Then there was a newfangled thing called a can opener. You more or less affixed it to the container's rim, then pressed down in one swift motion, making sure not to jiggle the can and its contents too much while doing it. Beer showers were easy to come by! Once you got the hang of it, it wasn't bad, but it sure felt strange at first.

Yet we muddled through. Being tough in the clutch has always been an American tradition. America's beer drinkers were not about to take a vacation from that tradition. No sir, with beer can in one hand and beer can opener in the other, the beerophiles of America, east and west, north and south, sallied forth with beer can in one hand and beer can opener in the other, successfully opening cans and quenching thirsts.

These were proud moments in U.S. beer packaging — and drinking — history.

"THE TALK OF THE NATION." "The Talk of the Nation" — as stated on this 1935 point-of-purchase handout — may be a little far-fetched. But when the G. Krueger Brewing Co. of Newark placed its beer and ale for sale in cans in early 1935, it was certainly the talk of the brewing industry. Many industry analysts and not a few brewers thought the whole idea little more than a gimmick. But while the doomsayers were busy chortling, customers were buying ... and other brewers soon decided maybe they'd better get on the stick, too.

TO OPEN. Various brewers included various "How to Open" instructions on their pioneer cans. All did their best to make it seem easy ... as indeed it certainly turned out to be!

ALL ABOARD. When national giant Pabst jumped aboard the can wagon in July 1935, the can's success was pretty much assured. Stacked here is a six-pack minus one of Pabst's earliest cans.

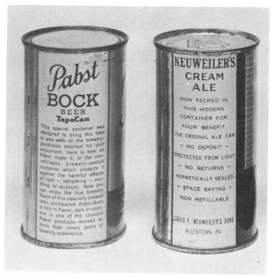

HERMETICALLY SEALED. When introduced, the beer can had to overcome more than how-to-open unfamiliarity. It had to overcome consumer skepticism as well. As a result early can copy was usually pretty hard-sell stuff. Every possible advantage of buying by the can was given ... right there on the can.

September 1936 *Brewery Age* ad

The Evolution of the Beer Can

1935 — The beer can is born. In January Krueger test-markets beer in cans in Richmond, Virginia.

1940 — Packaged beer — cans and bottles outsells draft beer for the first time.

1942/ All beer cans, over two billion

1946 — of them, are shipped overseas to our fighting forces.

1954 — Schlitz introduces the sixteen-ounce can.

1958 — Hawaii's Primo Brewing Co. comes out with the first aluminum cans in North America.

1962 — The Pittsburgh Brewing Co., brewers of Iron City Beer, introduces the tab-top can.

1969 — The beer can outsells the beer bottle for the first time in U.S. brewing history.

1970 — The Beer Can Collectors of America (BCCA) is formed in St. Louis.

1985 — The beer can celebrates its thirtieth birthday.

YOU'RE OUT/YOU'RE IN. 1964 ad from a Boston Red Sox program, extolling the as-yet-still-new pull top.

THE BOTTLE/CAN. Not all early beer cans were created equal. While beer makers were competing for beer sales, beer can makers were competing for can sales, so it was only logical that a can company came out with a variation on the beer can theme — a bottlelike top. Variously called a spout top, a cone top, a crown top, and cap-sealed, it did have certain advantages: it did not require a special opener, was more familiar to beer-in-bottle buyers, and, from the brewery's point of view, could be filled via their present bottling line.

But the bottle/can also had certain disadvantages: it was taller and thus took up more space in the refrigerator (as well as on store shelves and in delivery trucks) and because its opening was smaller, it took a brewer longer to fill than the flat-top can. Eventually the disadvantages outweighed the advantages . . . and the bottle/can went the way of the growler.

NO CAN-OPENING PROBLEMS FOR HIM. Once cans got going, it seemed as if everyone got into the act!

Circa 1936 postcard

How to Drink Beer

How to drink beer is a topic that would appear to be best resolved in one short sentence: open your mouth wide, pour in, enjoy. End of short sentence. End of topic. And generally that does work fine.

But there's *drinking* beer and there's *really enjoying drinking* beer. So Let's pretend this is Beer Drinking 101. You're the student. I'm the prof. Here's what I'd tell you.

Lesson A – Buy Fresh

Beer is a very temperamental beverage. It's sensitive . . . to heat, to light, to extreme cold, to just sitting on the shelf. It starts to break down fairly soon after it's been packaged, so don't buy bottles or cans that look as if they've been sitting around awhile. And steer way clear of any beer that appears as if it could've been exposed to sunlight and/or heat.

Your palate will appreciate you for it.

Lesson B – Store Well

Obviously Lesson A applies here, too. Do not store beer — be it in bottles or cans — where it's exposed to heat, sunlight, or extreme cold. Never put it in the freezer, even if for a few minutes. Keep it in a cool, dark place. A basement is fine; so is your refrigerator. To minimize the amount of

STORE WELL. Here's a good example of how and where *not* to store beer. Keep it like this, next to a hot radiator, and it's almost bound to taste bad, somewhat "skunky."

beer exposed to the air within the bottle or can, store it standing upright.

Your beer will appreciate you for it.

Lesson C – Pour Properly

When the moment of truth comes, pour your beer gently into your glass or mug and right down the middle, *not* down the

BUY FRESH. Never buy any beer that's been sitting in a store window, even if it's as pretty a display as this. Chances are that's all it's good for . . . sitting in a display. (Photo courtesy Photography Collection, Harry Ransom Humanities Research Center, University of Texas at Austin)

Circa 1930 San Antonio window display

Crab boil, Raceland, Louisiana, 1938

DO POUR. Yep, our lady friend here was a dandy alright, drinking right out of the bottle at the old crab boil. Trouble is, between the crabs and the carbon dioxide, she may still be suffering from indigestion to this day. (Photo courtesy Library of Congress)

side. By pouring it down the middle you produce a full head, and that's what you want to do. It enhances the beer's full bouquet while allowing its carbon dioxide gasses to escape.

Your body will appreciate you for it.

Lesson D – Do Pour

Do pour your beer into a glass, mug, or whatever. Sure, tough guys (and gals, too) drink their brew right out of the can or bottle, but the chances are they're gassy guys (and gals, too) as a result. Beer is a highly gaseous mixture of grains and yeast. It needs to be poured to allow the bouquet to build ... and the gasses to escape.

Your family and friends will appreciate you for it.

Lesson E – Drink Warmer

Most of us drink our beer too darned cold. Beer is a beverage of flavor. The more it's chilled, the more the flavor is throttled and the more you're robbed of beer's full taste. Try serving your beer at fifty or fifty-five degrees or so. What this most likely translates to is: about ten or fifteen minutes prior to pouring your beer, take it out of the refrigerator and allow it to warm up. Or serve it at "cellar temperature" (i.e., right out of the basement).

Your taste buds will appreciate you for it.

Lesson F – Don't Guzzle

Chug-a-lugging your beer gets you nothing but a good shot at heartburn and less than the full enjoyment from your brew. Drink your beer slowly; savor it; almost chew it. You'll be surprised at how much more you really like it, how much richer it tastes. Your digestion — and your sense of enjoyment — will thank you for it.

That's really all there is to it. Follow these lessons, plus the hints contained in The Care and Feeding of Beer Glasses, pages 36–37 and you'll find yourself graduating from Beer Drinking 101 to Beer Enjoyment 101. There is a difference!

Circa 1948 Trommer's sign

DRINK WARMER. "Ice Cold" looks nice and sounds nice ... but I'll bet you that just slightly cool will taste a heck of a lot better.

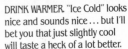

Circa 1950 comic postcard

POUR PROPERLY. Our boy here is smarter than he may appear: he obviously poured his bottle of ale right down the middle of the mug, producing a nice, full head and giving all those gasses a chance to escape. He looks more content for it already.

DON'T GUZZLE. Is this man guzzling or is this man guzzling? If he is, he's making a mistake. Slow your beer right on down; enjoy it a whole lot more. (Photo courtesy *The San Antonio Light* Collection, Institute of Texan Cultures, San Antonio, Texas)

Circa 1935 bartender, San Antonio

111

Malt-ified Movies

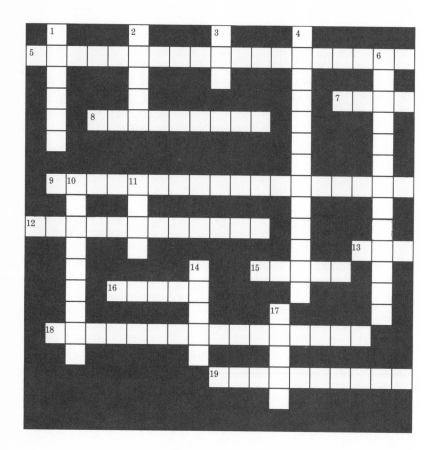

(Answers are on page 116.)

So you think you know your movie classics! Well, you've never known them like this. With the change of a letter or two (or three or four), each movie's *title* becomes beer-ified. It'll shock movie purists . . . but it's fun.

Note: Most of the movie titles really are classics, the type of flicks that regularly play in revival houses and film festivals across the country. The few nonclassics are so noted.

Good luck!

Across

5. Kirk Douglas and E. G. Marshall were the leading players in this 1961 story of four American soldiers on trial for rape. Definitely a nonclassic, perhaps now best remembered for its title song, sung by Gene Pitney. Pittsburghers will have an easy go of this one.

7. This spy thriller was directed not once but twice by Alfred Hitchcock. The 1934 version starred Leslie Banks, Edna Best, and Peter Lorre; the 1956 version, James Stewart and Doris Day. *The Man Who_____Too Much.*

8. Vivien Leigh won an Academy Award and Marlon Brando made his mark in this 1951 adaptation of a Tennessee Williams play: *A Streetcar Named_____.* Played big in northeastern Pennsylvania.

9. This 1953 classic established Frank Sinatra as someone who could act as well as sing. Also starred Burt Lancaster, Deborah Kerr, Donna Reed, Montgomery Clift, and Ernest Borgnine.

12. This 1930 German film shot Maria Magdalene Von Losch (better known as Marlene Dietrich) to stardom. A 1959, far less successful, version starred May Britt.

13. Claudette Colbert, George Brent, and Robert Young were featured in this 1949 romantic comedy, a semiclassic at best: *Bride for _____.*

15. A delightful farce, 1943 style, with Jean Arthur, Joel McCrea, and Charles Coburn in the leading roles: *The _____ the Merrier.*

16. Also a 1943 movie, this suspense thriller was shot on location in Santa Rosa, California. Directed by Alfred Hitchcock, it starred Teresa Wright as the unsuspecting niece and Joseph Cotten as her to-be-suspected uncle: *Shadow of a _____.*

18. Preston Sturges had to be included here somewhere . . . and here he is as director of this 1944 romp about an army reject who becomes a hometown hero. Eddie Bracken, William Demarest,

and Ella Raines starred:_____ _____
_____ *Hero.*

19. Alfred Hitchcock's back for his third
and last appearance as director of this
1954 gripper that had James Stewart
and Grace Kelly in the leading roles,
with Raymond Burr as the heavy.

Down

1. A Swedish maid becomes politically
important in this 1947 flick that featured
a leading cast of Loretta Young, Joseph
Cotten, Ethel Barrymore, and Charles
Bickford: *The Farmer's* _____.

2. I would not call this a classic, but no
retitling is needed either. This 1947
Bing Crosby and Dorothy Lamour musical is also the name of New Orleans's
favorite beer.

3. Paul Newman, Patricia Neal, Melvyn
Douglas, and Brandon de Wilde wrestle
with Texan heat and each other in this
1963 saga. It's appropriate: Paul Newman
is reputedly quite fond of our new title.

4. A comedy classic if ever there were one,
this Billy Wilder–directed 1959 film spar-
kled with Marilyn Monroe, Jack Lemmon,
Tony Curtis, and Joe E. Brown.

6. Sam Spade is on the job in this 1941
Dashiell Hammett whodunit. All-star
cast included Humphrey Bogart, Mary
Astor, Sidney Greenstreet, Peter Lorre,
Gladys George, Ward Bond, and others.
It was actually a redo—but much
more brilliantly done—of a 1931 movie of
the same name.

10. This is one of those to-be-forgotten spec-
taculars that popped up with titanic
casts—and budgets to match—during
the fifties and sixties, always starring
Charlton Heston. This one, shot in Utah
because it resembled Palestine more
than Palestine did, also included
Dorothy Malone, Max Von Sydow, David
McCallum, Claude Raines, Sidney
Poitier, Sal Mineo, Carroll Baker, Ed
Wynn, Shelley Winters, Telly Savalas,
Angela Lansbury, Jose Ferrer . . . and

John Wayne in a one-sentence role.
Don't be surprised if you Miss this one:
*The Greatest Story Ever*_____.

11. This timeless Shakespeare tragedy is
certainly best known as a play, but it
was made into a film in 1970. Shakespeare's father was an ale conner—an
official who tasted brews to make sure
they were up to snuff—so he just might
like our new title (though I sure wouldn't
want to bet on it!): *King*_____.

14. Made first as a silent movie and twice
as a talkie, this is probably the most
famed of the many French Foreign
Legion dramas. Telly Savalas, Guy
Stockwell, Doug McClure, Leslie Nielsen,
and Leon Gordon starred in the newer
(1966), more violent version, while Gary
Cooper, Ray Milland, Robert Preston,
Brian Donlevy, and J. Carrol Naish
braved it out in the earlier (1939), more
romantic go: _____ *Geste.*

17. Goldie Hawn as the waif, and Peter
Sellers as the sex-on-his-mind television personality, romped their way
through this 1970 British comedy:
There's a _____ *in My Soup.* Texas
beer lovers—or lovers of Texas beer
—will be able to rattle off the answer
to this one about as quickly as they can
wolf one down.

"Give an Irishman lager for a month,
and he's a dead man. An Irishman is
lined with copper, and the beer cor-
rodes it. But whiskey polishes the
copper and is the saving of him."
—*Mark Twain*
Life on the Mississippi, 1883

Hopsy Hits

Crossword #2

Here's your second chance for the Beer Crossword Puzzle Hall of Foam. Nineteen popular songs, representing several generations of musical preference, have been herein "beer-ized." So pour yourself a foamy one, put some sounds on the record player or tape deck, and see how well you do with Beer Crossword Puzzle #2: Hopsy Hits.

(Answers are on page 116.)

Across
1. Dylan's "Like a Rolling _____."
4. One of *the* smash hits of WWII, the Andrews Sisters' "Don't Sit under the _____ with Anyone Else But Me."
9. Carl Perkins wrote and recorded the original (and best!) version of this great fifties rocker: "You Can Do Anything You Want, but Baby, Lay offa Them Blue Suede _____."

11. On a hot summer night in Texas, Mick and the Stones might well find themselves longing for "Some _____" rather then "Some Girls."
13. Foreigner was far from alone when they admitted "I Want to _____ _____ Love Is."
14. Every month there should be at least one "Ruby Brews _____."
17. Not surprisingly, we've changed "When You Wish upon a Star" to "When You Wish upon a _____ Star."
18. Even Taco wouldn't care about "Puttin' on the Ritz" when you can, instead, be "Puttin' on the_____."
19. This was a mid-sixties classic, Procol Harum's "A Whiter Shade of _____."

Down
2. Old standard time: "I Get No Kick from Champagne . . . but I Get a Kick _____ _____ _____."
3. Brooklyn's Little Anthony and the Imperials scored big with their plaintiff fifties ballad "_____ _____ _____ _____."
5. Out West Coast–way Prince and the Revolution could be tempted to alter their smash hit somewhat and sing about "_____ _____."
6. Screaming Jay Hawkins has been doing his thing rising out of a casket ever since he had a hit with this song in 1956.
7. Originally recorded by the Isley Brothers, this later became a Beatles success as well.
8. Plural of where Danny and the Juniors wanted to go: "Let's Go to the _____."
10. The Police hit the charts big in 1985 with "Every _____ _____ _____."
12. Especially for Oregon Beatles fans: "A Blitz-Weinhard _____ _____."
15. If Tony Orlando had been more of a beer aficionado, he'd probably have tied a _____ ribbon around the old oak tree.
16. Gloated Del Shannon when someone else hurt the girl that had hurt him: "_____ off to Larry."

Sudsy Sayings

Here's your third — and last — shot at Beer Crossword Puzzle famedom. If you're a master of wise sayings and timeless adages, this should be right up your alley. There are nineteen proverbs, adages, famous sayings, and the like all, of course, "beer-ized" for your crossword pleasure. One or two or more letters have been changed in order to work a beer brand or word into the saying.

Good luck and remember . . . if you're having problems, stick with it. After all, ale's well that ends well!

(Answers are on page 116.)

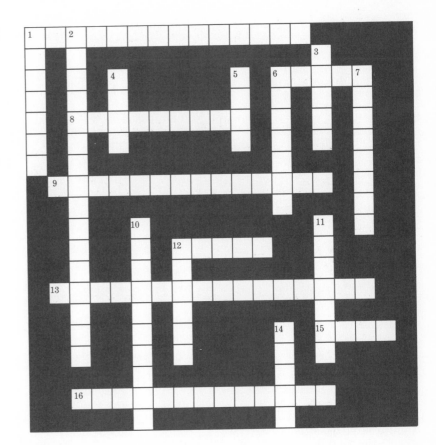

Across

1. The game's not over
   _____ _____ _____.
6. _____ _____fair in love and war.
8. _____ _____ _____, out of mind.
9. All that glitters _____ _____ _____.
12. Time _____all wounds.
13. It's an ill wind_____ _____ _____
    _____.
15. A rolling_____gathers no moss.
16. Last one in_____ _____
    _____ _____. (Knowing the nickname of a popular northeastern Pennsylvania brew helps with this one)

Down

1. _____ _____things in life are Genesee.
2. Harry S Truman: "_____ _____
   _____ _____."
3. Little pitchers have big _____.
4. _____makes right.
5. Mark Twain: "Don't go around saying the world owes you a living. The world owes you nothing. It was_____ first."
6. Good for what_____ _____.
7. Time waits for_____ _____.
10. There's no need to "beer-ize" this one, it's fine just as is:_____ _____ should not be tale tellers.
11. It never rains but_____ _____.
12. To make a long story_____.
14. Two wrongs do not make_____ _____.

> "Let people have good beer, and let them have it in the right way, in the home and in nice surroundings, and you'll hear a lot less about depression and despair."
> — *Col. Jacob Ruppert, January 1933*

Crossword Answers

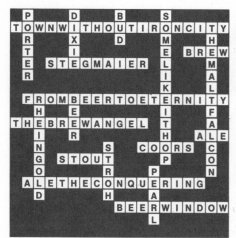

Malt-ified Movies

Let's have the real titles stand up, too . . .

Across

5. *Town Without Pity*
7. *The Man Who Knew Too Much*
8. *A Streetcar Named Desire*
9. *From Here to Eternity*
12. *The Blue Angel*
13. *Bride for Sale*
15. *The More the Merrier*
16. *Shadow of a Doubt*
18. *Hail the Conquering Hero*
19. *Rear Window*

Down

1. *The Farmer's Daughter*
2. *Dixie*
3. *Hud*
4. *Some Like It Hot*
6. *The Maltese Falcon*
10. *The Greatest Story Ever Told*
11. *King Lear*
14. *Beau Geste*
17. *There's a Girl in My Soup*

Hopsy Hits

And the real titles, too . . .

Across

1. *Like a Rolling Stone*
4. *Don't Sit under the Apple Tree with Anyone Else But Me*
9. *Blue Suede Shoes*
11. *Some Girls*
13. *I Want to Know What Love Is*
14. *Ruby Tuesday*
17. *When You Wish upon a Star*
18. *Puttin' on the Ritz*
19. *A Whiter Shade of Pale*

Down

2. *I Get a Kick out of You*
3. *Teardrops on My Pillow*
5. *Purple Rain*
6. *I Put a Spell on You*
7. *Twist and Shout*
8. *At the Hop*
10. *Every Breath You Take*
12. *A Hard Days Night*
15. *Tie a Yellow Ribbon*
16. *Hats off to Larry*

Sudsy Sayings

. . . and the sayings without the sudsyness.

Across

1. *The game's not over to the last out.*
6. *All is fair in love and war.*
8. *Out of sight, out of mind.*
9. *All that glitters is not gold.*
12. *Time heals all wounds.*
13. *It's an ill wind that blows no good.*
15. *A rolling stone gathers no moss.*
16. *Last one in is a rotten egg.*

Down

1. *The best things in life are free.*
2. *"The buck stops here."*
3. *Little pitchers have big ears.*
4. *Might makes right.*
5. *"Don't go around saying the world owes you a living. The world owes you nothing. It was here first."*
6. *Good for what ails you.*
7. *Time waits for no man.*
10. *Ale sellers should not be tale tellers.*
11. *It never rains but it pours.*
12. *To make a long story short.*
14. *Two wrongs do not make a right.*

> "What two ideas are more inseparable than beer and Britannia? What event more awfully important to an English colony than the erection of its first brewhouse?"
>
> —Rev. Sydney Smith
> Lady Holland

He Didn't Want to Paint the House Anymore

Most people, when they get tired of painting their house, either aluminum-side it or pay someone else to paint it. Not John Milkovisch. He became the "Beer Can House" man.

As his wife, Mary, explains it:

John started saving beer cans about twenty-two years ago, when Budweiser came out with aluminum cans. He cut the cans up because they fascinated him and were real colorful but hadn't decided what he was going to do with them. He cut the rims off the top and bottom and flattened out the rest.

He started putting them on the house about thirteen years ago. Actually he didn't want to paint the house anymore.

The cans he put on the house he put together with four-ounce aluminum tacks in sheets about thirty-six inches by thirty-six inches. He started out with a curtain of Budweiser cans across the driveway and just got carried away. He collected then any kind of cans that were aluminum, and friends and people gave him cans, and he also drinks six to eight cans a day and now drinks anything that's on special.

I thought he had lost his mind, but everyone seems to like it. And we've had people from England, Japan, Australia, and all over the U.S. Even the art professor from Rice University has been here several times and sends some of his students. They call it "art."

"LIKE A GIANT WIND CHIME." John Milkovisch's house at 222 Malone Street in Houston. In addition to having outer walls that are completely beer can-ized, the house is topped off — literally — with beer can tops (and bottoms). Mary: "The tops and bottoms are put together, some with steel pins, some with galvanized wire. These are the ones hanging from the roof. Some people say they sound like a giant wind chime when the wind blows."

The Case of the Missing Stolen Bases

During the 1985 St. Louis versus Kansas City World Series you may recall ex-baseball player Bobby Bonds doing a commercial for Miller Lite. In it, Bobby attests to having stolen 681 bases during his career. But Bobby was lite-footing it: he actually stole only 461. An embarrassed Miller yanked the commercial and redubbed it with the correct number of thefts. Moral: It's not a bad idea to check for liteness when it comes to larceny.

Jumping Joe Dugan, suffering from the heat at Babe Ruth's funeral in August 1948: "I'd give one hundred dollars for a beer."
Waite Hoyt: "So would the Babe."

117

Hops-in-the-Head Dubious Distinction Awards

It's time for the once-every-century Hops-in-the-Head Dubious Distinction Awards. Get ready to boo, to hoot, to hiss. Out of all the thousands and thousands of beer advertisements, packages, and photos through the years, we've done our foamiest to pick out the worst, the tackiest, the most "distinctive." These are all "10's" (or "8's" or "9's," anyway) . . . in the losing column.

The Opera Bar, LaCrosse, Wisconsin, 1915

San Francisco, May 14, 1975 (Photo courtesy of *San Francisco Examiner*)

And He'd Just Had It Washed

What are awards without an Oops Award? To Hamm's and to Duane Schultz, who parked his car in just the right place at just the right time, we present our Oopser. Although Duane's wheels looks a little worse for the wear, there appeared to be not a single bottle broken among the three thousand cases loaded in the overturned truck trailer. Score another one for beer.

Even the Spittoon Looks Smashed

The group of cohorts at the Opera Bar garners one of our more cherished awards, the Pie-eyed Award. Wanna bet their wives weren't too awfully glad to see them when they got home that night? (Photo courtesy Murphy Library, Special Collections and Area Research Center, University of Wisconsin, LaCrosse)

Hubert Fischer Brewery ad, 1900

Funny, It Sounds so Italian

The Overkill Award goes to the Hubert Fischer Brewery, Hartford, Connecticut. To name a beer Wurtz-Burger Burger Brau, whether it's "a real German Beer" or not, is a lot like naming a ballplayer Ty Cobb Willie Mays Babe Ruth. You more than get the idea.

Emmerling's ad, 1896

But Will It Help my Sex Life?

The Promise-It'll-Do-Everything Award goes to an oldie but goodie, John Emmerling's Brewery, Johnstown, Pennsylvania. Promised John: drink his beer, ale, or porter, and it'll do just about everything for you but grow hair.

Give Me Your Tired, Your Poor, Your Thirsty
On the front of the can was a portrait of John Adams looking like the handsome devil that he was, part of a colorful 1976 Bicentennial series put out by the Falstaff Brewing Corporation. But on the back of the can was a message from Paul Kalmanovitz, Falstaff's prexy and chairman of the board, and for it he wins the Tacky, Tacky Award. Being proud of America is fine; being proud of Falstaff Beer is okay, too . . . but implying that the two go hand in hand is indeed tacky, tacky.

Wilshire Boulevard and Grand Avenue, Los Angeles, March 1939

Circa 1948 Walter's label

What Else Would It Be?
The Stupidest Slogan Award goes to the Walter Brewing Company, Eau Claire, Wisconsin, for its 1940s "Beer That Is Beer" line. Actually, though, it didn't seem to hurt. Walter's remained in business long after most of its contemporaries, right through 1985, when it changed hands. The brewery is now known as Hibernia Brewing, Ltd., brewers of Hibernia Dunkelweizen Fest Beer.

So Was My Ex-Wife
The How-to-Lie-Though-Telling-the-Truth Award goes to the Golden West Brewing Co., Oakland, for "It's Starchless," the brewery's major advertising theme for many years in the 1930s and 1940s. So Golden Glow was starchless, so who cares? So was and is every other American beer. (Photo courtesy Department of Special Collections, University Research Library, UCLA)

But Does It Go with Watermelon?
To Louisville's Falls City Brewing Co. goes the Contrast Award. Their presumed strategy: an ad that would visually dramatize just how pale their Extra Pale was. (Photo courtesy University of Louisville Photographic Archives, Caufield & Shook Collection)

Falls City ad from 1939

Continued on next page

119

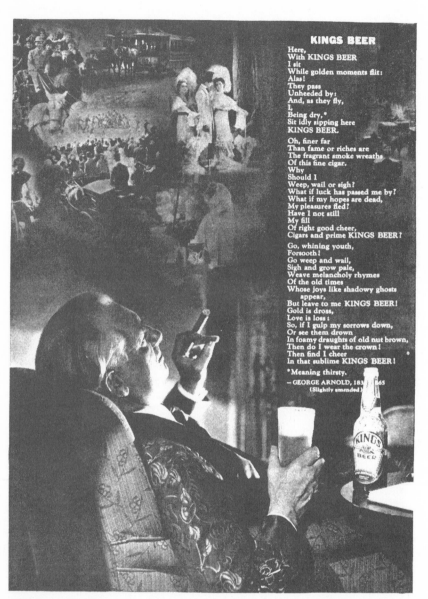

September 1933 ad for Kings Beer, the beer that was "Fit for Kings...and also Queens."

Circa 1952 supermarket display for Griesedieck Bros. Beer. "It's De-Bitterized!"

Trade Ya Two of My Flits for One of Yours

Winner of the Worst-Beer-Poem Award is Kings Brewery, Inc., Brooklyn. Beer poems do tend to be corny (maybe even ricey or hoppy?), but Kings' adaptation of "Beer," written over a century ago by George Arnold (1834–65), surpasses all cornfield boundaries. Flit, flit.

A Few Well-Chosen Words

The Foot-in-the-Mouth Award goes to one Rudolf Gull, who invented a special, patented beer de-bitterizing process used by Griesedieck Bros. Brewing Co., St. Louis, starting in 1950. Asked to explain his process, Rudolf had this to say: "My improved method makes it possible to produce beer of a superior quality, free from a coarse and bitter taste, in a closed fermenter, due to the fact that the major portion of the bitter sediment contained in the foam is separated from the foam and isolated at a point of position where it will not be subsequently acted upon, mixed with or redissolved in the fermenting wort, and my improved fermenter has the desirable characteristics of being easy to clean, of such design that the beer wort capacity of the apparatus is not reduced by the means employed to effect the separation and isolation of the bitter sediment contained in the foam, and it is of such construction tht the carbonic gases can be collected and the relatively small amount of beer which is carried out of the fermentation chamber into the foam chamber with the excaping gases, can be recovered and returned to the fermenting wort."

Got it?!

It Looks Like It Comes From a Deer Run

Let's give the Yucky Award to the Fred Koch Brewery, Dunkirk, New York, for the piles of mighty mysterious matter on its labels. The left-hand matter looks like French fries, but the right-hand could be hamburger meat, onion rings, garbage scrapings, or worse. Whatever it is — or was — the boys at the brewery liked it so much they put it on both their Golden Anniversary Beer and their Deer Run Pale Ale labels. Yum, yum.

Circa 1955 Koch's Labels

Pickin' up Those Bad Habits Again, eh Joe?

To Joe Charboneau goes the Bad-Beer-Manners Award. Charboneau attracted a lot of attention in 1980 when he cracked out 27 home runs, drove in 105 runs, and was voted the American League Rookie of the Year while playing for the Indians. But "Super Joe" also attracted attention for some of his more interesting habits, including swallowing uncooked eggs whole, devouring lighted cigarettes . . . and drinking beer through his nose. (Photo courtesy Cleveland Indians Co.)

Dixie Cafe matchbook covers. On the back is Meadville High's football schedule for 1940; but who ever got to the back with fronts like these?

Way Down South In Meadville, Pennsylvania

The Cornball Award could go to any one of the thousands of bars and beer joints across America that used girlie art matchbooks in the 1940s, but we're giving it to The Dixie Cafe, Meadville, Pennsylvania, for quantity as well as quality. Lenny Dixon, you old rogue.

Continued on next page

121

Emil Gaertner, circa 1940

... that makes GOLDEN GLOW

1934 Blumer Brewing Corporation ad for its Blumer's Golden Glow Beer

Altoona Brewing Co. brewhouse crew, circa 1940. Left to right: Frank Leonard, engineer; Larry Grieff, engineer; Frank Hokerl, assistant brewmaster; Frank Dirrigl, chief kettleman; Anton Gleixner, chief cellarman; George Epple, supt. bottling dept.

Smile and the Whole Brewery Smiles with You

To Emil Gaertner, brewmaster for the Altoona Brewing Co., Altoona, Pennsylvania, goes the Old Grouch Award. Being brewmaster is serious business, but it doesn't have to be grouchy business. You could have smiled at least a little for the camera, Emil. As it is it's hard to tell which looks worse, you or that blob of good stuff in front of you.

Let the Good Times Glow

The Blumer Brewing Corporation, Monroe, Wisconsin, comes in first in the race for the Honesty-Isn't-Always-the-Best-Policy Award. Sure, drinking beer makes you feel good and can give you a good glow, golden or otherwise. That's part of its charm; but to actually go out and advertise the fact . . . that's a no-no.

From the Brewers of Old Siesta Lager

The What-Me-Worry Award is split six ways among the entire brewhouse crew of the Altoona Brewing Co., Altoona, Pennsylvania. To look laid back is one thing . . . to look asleep at the brewhouse switch is another. Buck up, fellas, or we'll take away your beer-drinking privileges.

Porter: Pours Like Mud, Tastes Like Great

Men, Englishmen, too, have been heard of who do not know the taste of porter. This cannot be credited; though it may be readily believed that many are quite ignorant of the taste of water.
— *Westminster Review*, London, 1846

Pour out a glass of porter and you may well feel like you're pouring out a glass of mud. It's very definitely a dark beer and seems thicker, richer than "regular" beer. That's because it is. Porter is basically a dark ale, but it's heavier than traditional ale and it's sweeter, less hoppy, too. The roasted malt used in brewing it accounts for porter's dark, mudlike appearance.

Legend has it that porter's name came about in early eighteenth-century England. London's porters loved the dark brew so much that its name was changed from its then "entire butt" or "intire" to porter, in honor of its most ardent supporters. A second version has it that it was named porter because of its strength, a characteristic that all porters, be they in London or Luckenbach, must surely possess.

BEER-ALE-PORTER. This circa 1940 delivery truck from Shamokin, Pennsylvania's Fuhrman & Schmidt Brewing Co. reads "BEER-ALE-PORTER," as would've most all brew trucks from eastern Pennsylvania breweries not so many moons ago. That area of Pennsylvania — especially Philadelphia prior to Prohibition — was noted for its fine porters. Today at least one brewery in the Keystone State keeps alive the old tradition: Pottsville's D. G. Yuengling & Son rolls on with their Yuengling's Celebrated Pottsville Porter.

If you're ever in the Pottsville-Reading-Hazelton area, be sure to try it. Other than Yuengling's, your best bet for porter is one of the micros. It's not easy to find, but seek porter out and ye shall be darkly, thickly, and richly rewarded.

Pennsylvania porter labels from the 1930s and 1940s

A Beerwich on Rye and a Beer Nog, Please

Beer adds zest to life. It makes it fun to be thirsty. Beer also adds zest to food. It makes it fun to be hungry. Two cars in every garage and beer soup in every pot, as they say.

With that brilliantly delicious line as our opener, here's today's all beer meal.

WE'LL DRINK TO THAT. Who knows, maybe someday soon someone will invent beer ice cream. Why not?!

Beer Soup

2 large onions
2 tablespoons cooking oil
1 small clove garlic
1 quart beer or ale
beef bones, large quantity
1½ cups barley
¼ teaspoon white peppercorns
2 large carrots
1 small cabbage
1 tablespoon malt vinegar
¼ teaspoon Worcestershire sauce

Slice onions into rings and brown in oil with pieces of garlic in large soup pot. Add half the beer or ale, then the soup bones, barley, and peppercorns. Add water until the bones are covered; bring to a boil and let simmer for three to four hours. Dice carrots and add to soup. Slice cabbage and steam in separate pot with 1 tablespoon vinegar. Pour in rest of beer or ale and Worcestershire sauce. Add the cabbage. Simmer for another five minutes. Serve with chopped parsley or grated cheese. Serves 6.

Melon in Beer

1 medium-size honeydew melon
¼ pint (4 ounces) beer or ale
½ teaspoon cinnamon
4 tablespoons superfine granulated sugar

Chill the melon well. Cut into four wedges, remove seeds, and sprinkle well with beer or ale. Mix cinnamon and sugar together in a bowl and sprinkle over melon slices, too. Serve immediately. Serves 4.

Quiche Lorraine à la Bière

8 ounces shortcrust pastry, frozen or
*   homemade*
6 rashers streaky bacon
1 medium-size onion
1 ounce butter
1 egg
1 egg yolk
1 cup milk
½ cup beer or ale
2 tablespoons grated Cheddar cheese
seasoning to taste

Roll out pastry to one-quarter inch thick and line into baking pan. Dice bacon, slice onion into rings, and sauté together in butter in a frying pan until onion is soft but not brown. Meanwhile, mix egg, extra yolk, milk, and beer together in a bowl with the grated cheese. Pour contents of sauté pan, including what remains of the butter, into the other ingredients and mix well together. Pour into baking pan, making sure that the bacon and onion are fairly evenly distributed, and bake in a moderate oven, 350°F, for twenty-five to thirty minutes. Serves 4.

Zucchini in Beer

1 tablespoon cooking oil
1 clove garlic
4 medium-size zucchini
¼ pint (4 ounces) beer or ale
1 green pepper, seeded and chopped
¼ teaspoon salt
¼ teaspoon pepper
½ teaspoon basil
1 tablespoon chopped pimiento

Heat oil in saucepan and brown garlic lightly. Wipe and slice zucchini; add to pan and brown lightly. Add remaining ingredients, cover, and simmer for about twenty minutes or until zucchini are tender. Serves 2-3.

Beer Omelet

4 eggs
½ cup beer or ale
1 ounce butter
2 tablespoons grated Cheddar cheese

Lightly beat the eggs and the beer in a mixing bowl. Heat an omelet pan until very hot and drop in half the butter. Pour in half the egg and beer mixture and fork until fluffy. Cover with grated cheese. Fold over and let cook for a few seconds to allow cheese to melt. Serve on a hot plate. Serves 1-2.

Beerwich

4 slices white (or rye, if you're feeling
    adventuresome) bread
3 eggs
¾ cup beer or ale
1 tablespoon sugar
¼ teaspoon salt
2 tablespoons butter or oleomargarine
4 slices ham
4 slices Swiss or American cheese

Arrange bread in large baking dish. Beat eggs, beer, sugar, and salt until fluffy. Pour over bread, turning each slice to cover well. Heat butter in skillet. Carefully transfer bread to skillet. Cook over medium heat four minutes on each side or until golden brown. Put ham and cheese between bread slices. Serves 1-2.

Beer Burgers

1 pound beef, minced
½ medium-size onion, finely chopped
dash Worcestershire sauce
seasoning to taste
½ cup flour
½ cup beer or ale

Mix the beef thoroughly with the onion, seasoning, and Worcestershire sauce. Shape into thick burgers and roll in flour. Melt butter in frying pan and sprinkle with Worcestershire sauce. Make a hole in the top of each burger and fill with beer or ale.

Place in pan and fry. Beer will be absorbed into the burger by the time you are ready to cook the second side. Turn and cook second side to desired rareness. Serves 4.

Porter Plum Cake

½ pound butter or oleomargarine
1 pound flour
½ pound brown sugar
1 pound raisins or currants
¼ pound mixed dried peel
1 teaspoon baking soda
½ teaspoon cinnamon
½ teaspoon grated nutmeg
3 eggs
½ pint (8 ounces) porter or stout

Stir the butter, flour, and sugar together in a bowl until well mixed. Add the fruit, dried peel, baking soda, cinnamon, and nutmeg. Mix in the three eggs and gradually add the half pint of porter or stout. If mixture appears to be getting too wet, do not use all of it. Pour into well-buttered cake tin and bake in a moderate oven, 325°F, for 2½ hours.

Apple Dragons

4 large cooking apples
2 ounces brown sugar
2 ounces white raisins, chopped
1 ounce butter
¼ pint (4 ounces) beer or ale

Wash and core apples and place in a shallow baking dish. Mix together sugar and raisins and butter and pile into center of apples. Pour over beer or ale and sprinkle a little more sugar in the beer that's in the bottom of the baking dish. Bake in oven at 375°F for forty-five minutes to an hour. Serve hot with a little of the syrup spooned over. Serves 4.

ON THE RUN. They'll all come running for your Zucchini in Beer.

Continued on next page

125

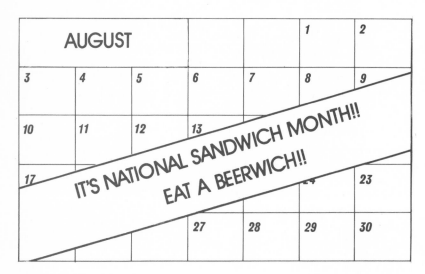

NATIONAL SANDWICH MONTH. The Beerwich was invented in 1954 by Frank Kohler, author of the then nationally syndicated column "The Skillet Club For Men," as part of National Sandwich Month in August.

THEY'LL LOVE IT. Make your next party a Beer Burger and Shandy Gaff party. Your guests will love you for it.

Beer Nog

1 cup rum
½ cup sugar
1½ pints (24 ounces) stout
4 eggs

Mix the rum, sugar, and stout in a saucepan. Bring to a boil and simmer five minutes. Remove from heat. Beat the eggs in a bowl and gradually add the beer mixture, stirring steadily to prevent curdling. Allow to chill in the refrigerator for at least two hours. Before serving, beat with a rotary beater. Serves 2-3.

Shandy Gaff

½ pint (8 ounces) chilled beer or ale
½ pint (8 ounces) chilled ginger ale

Pour the beer and ginger ale simultaneously into a chilled glass. Serves 1.

For other beer-based beverages, including the likes of Tewahdiddle, Figgy Sue, and Syllabub, see Beer Concoctions on page 14. And don't forget the favorite with almost any meal—plain, good old beer. Add nuts—Beer Nuts, of course—and you have it—today's all-beer meal.

Most of the recipes in our all-beer meal are from Carole Fahy's excellent book *Cooking with Beer* (Dover Publications, New York, 1978). It's worth tracking down a copy.

> "She brews good ale—and thereof comes the proverb, 'Blessing of your heart, you brew good ale.'"
>
> —*Shakespeare*
> *The Two Gentlemen of Verona*

126

Beer and Religion: Not Bad Bedfellows

Everybody gets thirsty and, as this 1959 view of the Little Sisters of the Poor in Louisville would indicate, nuns are no exception. Although this inside-a-beer-pantry — and a well-stocked one at that — scene may seem strange, it shouldn't. In Europe numerous religious orders have, through the ages, not only enjoyed beer but brewed it as well. And, of course, it was in a monastery in Budweis, Czechoslovakia, that Budweiser first saw the light of day (see page 153).

In America we've tended to pay homage to religious brewing more via brand names than via actual brewing. The Independent Brewing Co. of Pittsburgh brewed a near beer they called Old Monastery in 1933 and 1934. An Old Abbey Beer was brewed by the Old Abbey Brewing Co. of Chicago from 1935 to 1941. And Buffalo's William Simon Brewing Co. brewed an Old Abbey Ale for forty years, from 1933 to the year the brewery closed, 1973. Plus there have been numerous different Friars Ales and Beers and even a Friars Malt Liquor, produced by the Friars Ale Brewing Co., Port Huron, Michigan, from 1944 to 1953.

There has been, though, at least one instance of an actual brewery within a religious order in the United States, and it's a noteworthy instance. In 1844 Father Boniface Wimmer arrived in America from Munich and established the first Benedic-

(Photo courtesy of University of Louisville Photographic Archives: Royal Studio Collection)

tine community in the United States, the St. Vincent Abbey, in Beatty (near Latrobe, the home of today's Rolling Rock Beer), Pennsylvania. He brought with him six priests and several lay brothers. The next year twenty-three more brothers made their way from Germany to the prospering abbey on the banks of the Loyalhanna River.

The community continued to grow, but one thing was missing: the beer the monks had so enjoyed in their native Germany. To solve this dry spell, Father Wimmer secured the permission of the Pope in 1885 to make beer solely for the consumption of the brothers. The beer they brewed, however, was so good that its fame spread outside the abbey's walls, and Father Wimmer was persuaded to allow his beer to be sold in selected outlets throughout Pennsylvania. It was advertised in secular newspapers, bottled by a Pittsburgh bottling firm, and its reputation growing evermore respected when, alas, Prohibition forces, especially within the Catholic church, caused the beer to be taken off the public market in 1899. Bye-bye St. Vincent Abbey beer.

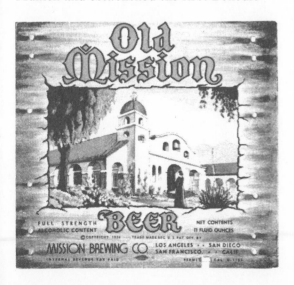

FROM OLD ABBEY TO OLD MONASTERY TO OLD MISSION. Old Mission Beer was a West Coast standby from 1934 until 1965. Now it's just a collector's item.

127

Lager: It's the Biggie of American Beer

Lager, in German, means to store, to age. As with Scotch whiskey and fine wines, it benefits from being properly seasoned. Lager is a traditionally German drink, brought to our shores about 1840. No one knows for certain, but John Wagner is generally credited with being the first to successfully brew lager in America. Wagner, a Bavarian immigrant, brewed up a batch in back of his house on St. John Street, near Poplar, in Philadelphia in 1840.

From such humble beginnings, lager's popularity grew like topsy. Fueled by successive waves of German immigration from the 1840s onward, lager steadily overtook ale and porter in popularity. But it wasn't only the newly arrived German-Americans who drank it. Americans of just about every background were taken with lager's tangy, effervescent, and lively taste.

Today lager accounts for well over 90 percent of all malt beverage sales in America. Even John Wagner would be impressed.

Circa 1895 postcard

1898 California advertisement

AGE MAKES THE DIFFERENCE. Although ale is top fermented and is ready for consumption almost immediately after brewing, lager beer is bottom fermented and has to be aged before serving.

It's the aging that makes the difference in a good lager. 'Twas so seemingly eons ago when Grand Prize was "Texas' Largest Seller" (Grand Prize hasn't even been brewed since 1963), and it's still so today.

Circa 1948 matchbook

1879 New York advertisement

COAST TO COAST. Well before the century had turned, lager bier (or beer, as it came to be Anglicized) had become America's favorite. How could it not have, with adjectives such as "renowned, healthy and most palatable" or "healthful, pure and unadulterated"? Here was, indeed, a beverage "to your very good health."

128

THE BIG CHILL. There's hardly an old-time lager beer brewery that wasn't built into the side of a hill in one way or another. That's because lager not only has to be aged, it has to be aged at a cool temperature. And in the days before artificial refrigeration came into being (the 1880s), storage in underground caves was the only surefire way of achieving the necessary big chill. It didn't take German-American ingenuity long to figure out that if your brewhouse were built into a hill, you'd have to dig less far underground to get underground caves.

Galena, Illinois' Fulton Brewery, pictured nestled into the side of the prerequisite hill in this circa 1875 view, still stands today, and it's still nestled into the side of a hill. Although its lagering days are long over, the majestic old brewery's caves are yet in use. Today they hold pottery and stoneware for several of the shops that make up the Fulton Brewery Market, an antiquey-craftsy indoor mall. It's a fitting use of the beautiful old brewery in a town that's as antiquey-craftsy — and as beautiful — as Galena.

What a Way to Go

I feel no pain dear mother now
But oh, I am so dry!
O take me to a brewery
And leave me there to die.
— *Anonymous*

129

What to Look for in a Bar

There is nothing which has yet been contrived by man by which so much happiness is produced as by a good tavern or inn.
— *Samuel Johnson, 1709–1784*

The Bar Tourists of America is an organization, formalized in 1981, that conducts imbibing forays in various locales across this great land. Most of the imbibing is beer . . . as well it should be! The BTA group, anywhere from fifteen to forty strong, visits seven to fifteen select bars, taverns, beer parlors, or joints during the better part of a day . . . and sometimes well into the better part of the evening, too. Forays — or tours — have been held in such far-flung places as Boston, Baltimore, Hoboken, Allentown, Trenton, Berkeley/Oakland, and Marietta, Ohio.

The key word in Bar Tourists of America is not "America," however, and it's not "Tourists." It's "Bar." So here, condensed from official reports of the BTA, is what they look for in selecting which select bars to honor with their presence. You don't have to be part of a group, however, or be hanging around Hoboken or Trenton either, to reap the benefits of their advice. It's good, basic stuff.

Bars with men's names (Al's, Ben's, etc.) are good bets, as are places with "Haus" in the name. Bars with "Il," "El," "Le," or "La" are no good, nor are bars with numbers in the name, such as "121 Club" or the like. Bars with "Ye Olde" are hard to predict and should be checked out. Any place with the word "Cafe" in the name is usually good. There are no discos with "Cafe" in the name.

Once you get on the road, interesting bars are easy to spot. If the beer neon has an interesting brand, stop in. An old-looking place should be checked out. Surprisingly, you should stop in places that have been remodelled on the outside. Many old bars will put up aluminum siding on the outside, but keep the inside intact. Avoid any bar with more than one motorcycle parked outside.

Once inside, you can save time and money by walking out of any bar that is dominated by a pool table, serves only Bud in bottles, or is hostile. Eliminate the formica-top or post-war stainless steel type bars. Try to avoid the nouveau-antique "fern bar" types. Don't be hesitant to walk into a bar that has a teenybopper crowded atmosphere on a Friday night, for on a Saturday afternoon it might be a quiet place patronized by a handful of people. Once you find bars with potential, note the important features:

1. Backbar and bar, front door, other interesting or unusual features
2. Brands of beer on draught
3. Juke box — old or new songs on it
4. Historic or other features
5. Location and parking

Prosit!

CHEERIO. Cheerio . . . but be wary of ferns, formica, and bikers wisely warns the BTA.

**Some say we'll have rain—some snow—
But I know what I'm having—cheerio.**

SALOON BAR

The Bar Tourists of America currently has over three hundred active members — male and female. For information about joining, please see page 157.

Rave Reviews
Some typically candid BTA from-the-front-line barroom reviews:

Boston: "Next stop was Picadilly Filly, a downstairs bar almost devoid of decor. The itinerary said: 'the new owners promise some surprises.' They certainly did; one of them was the odor! The joint smelled as if someone had just blown lunch. One of the group, giving them the benefit of the doubt, said it might have been the paint they used, but I have to wonder. They did, however, treat us to the products of San Francisco's Anchor Brewery, Anchor Porter and Liberty Ale, which helped ease the assault on our nostrils."

Baltimore: "We next traveled to Carey St., between Pratt and McHenry, for the B & O Tavern. But don't expect some cutesy railroad motif. The joint is basically dingy. The restrooms haven't been cleaned since the last Bar Tour, but the service was courteous and friendly and the beers cheap. A sign over the backbar warns: 'No Bums Allowed,' making some of our group a tad uneasy, but we all seemed to meet the bar's admission criteria."

Penndel, Pennsylvania: "Next, the Tour moved on to Penndel, Pa. and Phil's Place. One P.M. was the perfect time to visit this bar, as any later hour might be suicidal. You see, Phil's is a classic biker bar. There were a few sleazy denizens in attendance at this early hour, but fortunately we outnumbered them. Bartender Grace Taylor got a real charge out of our group. I guess we were quite a departure from the norm around there."

And last but not least, from the banks of the mighty Muskingum . . .

Marietta, Ohio: "Judd's Bar, the next stop, was a no-nonsense, blue-collar bar. Nothing fancy here; not a fern in sight. It's a place to drink, not a place to go to be seen.

"Riverside Cafe, a semi-cowboy bar with punch-out holes in the men's room, was the next stop. It's a very dark, fifties-style, typical small town watering hole. You won't find many Guccis resting on the bar here. The Riverside does have the best juke box in town.

"The Keg Room is another working-man's bar, with a bowling alley above, sounding like a constant thunderstorm. Good pizza was available for the hungry Tourists, served by a sweet old lady who was later seen lugging kegs out back. The thirsty Tourists could choose from among eight tap beers — tops in town. The Keg Room is a little too bright, but pleasant."

Special thanks to BTA newsletter editor Jack McDougall for allowing me to use the above material. Jack, may all your bars — and your beers — be good ones!

LOCATION, LOCATION, LOCATION. They say that with real estate the important thing is location, location, location. Well location — the bar and its atmosphere — is a biggie in terms of true beer-quaffing enjoyment, too!

That's a Lot of Honor
Famed British novelist Graham Greene has beer as well as ink in his blood. Graham, King and Sons Brewery — in St. Edmunds outside London — was founded by his great-grandfather Benjamin Greene. When the author celebrated his eightieth birthday, in 1984, the brewery celebrated right along with him by brewing up one hundred thousand bottles of special beer in his honor.

Where It All Happens:
Macungie, Pennsylvania

Ah, the sweet sights and sounds of spring: the first robin, the crack of the bat, daffodils and forsythia . . . and Macungie, Pennsylvania.

Breweriana buffs come in all sizes and shapes, and for the better part of a decade they've been coming to the small eastern Pennsylvania village of Macungie in late March/early April. That's when the Eastern Coast Breweriana Association (ECBA) holds the first of its several yearly breweriana get-togethers, kind of a combined beer flea market and in-moderation beer blast. It's a fun event, with people adding to or thinning out their collection, making new acquaintances or renewing old ones, exchanging breweriana stories (which can often be akin to fish stories), enjoying a beer or two, and so on. *From Beer to Eternity* was delighted to be there for the Spring 1986 kickoff, April 5.

EIGHT MILES SOUTHWEST OF ALLENTOWN. Macungie is about eight miles southwest of Allentown, down route 100 four or so miles from Stroh's ultramodern fire-brewing facility. One of the village's outstanding features, along with friendly people and a lovely main street, is its Town Park Memorial Hall, where ECBA has held its spring breweriana get-together and trade session since the early 1980s. .

```
          E C B A
      SPRING  TRADE  MEET
DATE : SAT. APRIL 5 1986
TIME : 9 A.M. - 3 P.M. OPEN TO PUBLIC 11-3
PLACE : MACUNGIE MEMORIAL HALL, MACUNGIE, PA
COST : $8. PER TABLE — ONE TABLE PER MEMBER
       $2.00 FOR EACH ADD'L GUEST
INCLUDES : COFFEE + DOUGHNUTS IN A.M.
           BEER + SODA FROM 11-3
           FOOD, INCLUDING BREAKFAST, WILL BE
           AVAILABLE ON THE PREMISES.
TABLES CAN NOT BE GUARANTEED UNLESS
RESERVATION + MONEY IS RECEIVED PRIOR TO MARCH 23RD
   NO   SPECIAL   REQUESTS
```

AN INVITATION TO FUN. It's certainly not a fancy invitation, but it's a fun invitation. Just turn at Salvatore's Pizza . . . and be ready for a real good time.

Memorial Hall exterior

Memorial Hall interior

Ed Theberge, Warren, Rhode Island: "I'm looking for the odd New England piece, or Rhode Island piece, that might be down here in Pennsylvania. My son started collecting beer cans in 1976, so I joined with him and then subsequently started to get off into breweriana. This is the second time I've been down here and I've enjoyed myself. Again, it's more of the thrill that something hopefully will pop up."

"FULL OF GOOD CHEER." Nancy probably wouldn't get too excited about this circa 1940 Atlantic Company matchbook… but you never know.

Atlantic was for many years, from the thirties through the fifties, a major force in southern brewing, with plants in Atlanta, Chattanooga, Charlotte, Orlando, and Norfolk brewing the beer that was "Full of Good Cheer."

Gary Nowlin, with friends Joy and Nathan Hunsicker, Allentown, Pennsylvania: "I come to meet people like you. It's fun. I collect Pabst breweriana. Many years ago I was given a [Pabst] sign by a beer distributor, and I had been a Pabst drinker in college. I put the sign in my den, and I started collecting Pabst stuff. And I've stuck with it since."

Commented Joy: "I'm impressed. It's a nice show; there's a lot of different things."

And Nathan: "It's better than I thought."

Tom Hug, Lorain, Ohio: "What brings me to Macungie, Pa.? Good-quality beer advertising and to see old friends, old acquaintances that we haven't seen in a long time. We drove eight hours last night, but it's worth it. We have a good time."

Nancy Kim, Columbia, South Carolina: "I came here for Pennsylvania breweriana. Originally I'm from New York and a friend that I travel with is from Pennsylvania, so we collect anything from Pennsylvania. And we collect Atlantic Brewery items from the South. I've been collecting about five years. It's a lot of fun."

Continued on next page

GIVE ME A COLD SHAKESPEARE. Here's a piece of breweriana Tom, Hamp, and Nancy would all appreciate, a 1908 lithographed calendar from Philadelphia's Weisbrod & Hess Brewing Co., brewers of Rheingold and Shakespeare Beers.

Sue and Hamp Miller, Flemington, New Jersey: "We come to do a little selling and, who knows, maybe buying of old-time breweriana: lithos, pre-Prohibition items, anything turn of the century. We started collecting in 1973. We do this as a couple. We also enjoy the fellowship. There's a nucleus of people, probably twenty or thirty couples over time, that we've met and you see only a couple of times a year at these trade sessions. It's great fun!"

Don Cooper, Wildwood, New Jersey: "I was here as a visitor last year and I came up and decided to set up a table this year. I want to add to my collection. I'm into Anheuser-Busch tap knobs. I've been collecting about twelve years."

IT'S A GOOD CLUB. As Lowell and Joyce would undoubtedly be glad to tell you, the name *Utica Club* was first used for a line of soft drinks put out by Utica's West End Brewing Co. in 1919. It wasn't used as a beer brand name until after repeal, in 1933. (Coaster used with permission from the F.X. Matt Brewing Club)

Joyce and Lowell Owens, Utica, New York: "I work for a brewery, West End [Matt's] in Utica. I come to Macungie for the fun of trading, to see what else I can buy for my collection. I mostly collect Utica Club advertising. Actually we do it as a husband-wife team, been doing it for fifteen years. We enjoy the fellowship, meetin' all the rest of the collectors."

"IT'S BLENDED...IT'S SPLENDID!" Gary and the legendary Eddie Cantor would most likely have agreed on many things, not the least of which was Pabst: "It's Blended...It's Splendid."

135

Beerbusters

So you think you know your beer lore and facts. Well, here's your chance to prove — or disprove — it. We've come up with twenty questions — some tough, some not so tough — that should be fun regardless of how well you do.

The answers are just a couple of pages away. No peeking, though, until you've tried your hand at all twenty.

1. What reference book with a beer brand name as part of its title regularly sells a million copies a year?

2. Why did the Pilgrims land at Plymouth Rock?

3. What is the origin of the phrase "Mind your p's and q's"?

4. What do the Brooklyn Bridge and Piel's Beer have in common?

5. George Washington had a great fondness for the type of ale known as _____.

6. What is the derivation of the word *bridal*?

7. The word *pub* is a shortened version of _____ _____.

8. Beer is approximately
   (a) 72 percent,
   (b) 82 percent, or
   (c) 92 percent water?

9. Who wrote the following absolutely abysmal poem as part of a high school English IV assignment in 1958?

   Are you feeling great, the time when life is so dear?
   Then enjoy life even more, and, whatever you do, drink Schaefer beer.
   Are you feeling a little low? Well, have no fear,
   You'll soon feel better, and, whatever you do, drink Schaefer beer.
   Are you feeling absolutely miserable, as if the grave were near?
   Just have faith, and, whatever you do, drink Schaefer beer.
   Are you lying in state and the grave is here?
   Well, it's too late now, so, whatever you do, drink Schaefer beer.

10. What famous stage/screen/TV actress is, in real life, a brewer's daughter?

136

11. "Tonight, Let It Be _____."

12. What was the first paved street in North America ... and what did it have to do with beer?

13. Priestley's theories on oxygen were formulated while watching bubbles rise to the surface in a _____ _____ _____.

14. Using a beer rinse to give extra body to the hair was quite the rage forty years ago. It was was called a _____.

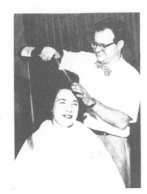

Pouring on the beer, 1947

15. "Brewed expressly for and with the personal approval of one of America's all-time great beer drinkers" characterized what (in)famous beer of the late 1970s?

16. One of *the* smash song hits of 1954/55 was "Mr. Sandman," sung by a female vocal quartet called the Chordettes. They got their start by being sponsored by the then-active _____ Breweries, Manitowoc, Wisconsin.

17. Anheuser-Busch started using its famed team of Clydesdales for promotional purposes in the (a) 1890s, (b) 1930s, (c) 1950s.

The Clydesdales doing their thing in the Big Apple, 1952 (Photo courtesy Anheuser-Busch Archives)

18. The only state that's never had an active brewery is _____.

19. The voices of Bert and Harry (Piel) belonged to none other than _____ and _____.

20. "It's the Water" has long been the slogan for _____ Beer.

The Bert and Harry sense of humor: biting but wonderful

The Chordettes as they appeared in 1949

Continued on next page

137

Beerbusters, Continued

Answers

1. *The Guinness Book of World Records*, originally undertaken by the venerable Dublin brewery to help settle barroom "discussions."

2. Because they were out of beer aboard the Mayflower. The Pilgrims' intended goal was much farther south, in Virginia, but they were forced to settle for the nearest suitable landing place. As recorded in the ship's log: "We could not now take time for further search or consideration; our victuals having been much spent, especially our beere."

3. In the English pubs of old, ale was sold in either *p*int or *q*uart tankards. The wise proprietor minded (i.e., kept track of) who had what of which; the wise customer did likewise.

4. Both the Brooklyn Bridge and Piel's opened for business on exactly the same day, May 24th, 1883. It was obviously a big day for Brooklyn. (Piel's was then located in the East New York section of Brooklyn. It is today brewed by Stroh's in Lehigh Valley, Pennsylvania.

5. The father of our country liked his *porter*. Whether or not that's the reason his cheeks always looked so red is unknown. What is known, however, is that there still exists a porter-brewing recipe written out in Washington's very own handwriting. It's among the collections of the New York City Public Library.

6. In seventeenth- and eighteenth-century jolly old England, special ales were brewed for many special occasions. Among these were ales brewed to honor the wedding day . . . and the bride. Called, naturally enough, bride's ale, this eventually became shortened to just "bridal."

7. Pub is short for Public House. It is British in origin.

8. Beer is 92 percent water. Ah, but what the other 8 percent does to it!

9. The author, with apologies all around to Schaefer, was Will Anderson. In other words, me. And I didn't even drink beer then. My teacher, Stan "The Man" Kramer, was not at all impressed. Commented he: "Poetry is not your forte — forced rhyme and irregular meter."

10. The brewer's daughter is Shirley Jones, whose acting career spans more than thirty years, starting in 1955, when the then twenty-one-year-old landed the female lead in the film adaptation of *Oklahoma*. Shirley's father, Paul Jones, was president of the still-very-much-in-existence Jones Brewing Co. of Smithton, Pennsylvania, from 1952 until his death in 1959.

11. "Tonight, Let it Be *Lowenbrau*": certainly one of beerdom's most melodic commercials, featuring the sweet vocal refrains of Arthur Prysock.

12. Stone Street in lower New York (then New Amsterdam) was paved in 1657 and was the first paved street in North America. Its paving was due to the several breweries located along its way: their delivery wagons, laden with beer, kept getting stuck in the mud.

13. Priestly was looking at the bubbles in a *vat of beer* in an English brewery when he came up with his theory of oxygen.

14. They were called *beerdos* and were so popular for a while that one brewery — the New Philadelphia Brewing Co., New Philadelphia, Ohio — even ceased, in 1949, its regular beer in favor of beer shampoo output.

15. The beer was "Billy." And the "all-time great beer drinker" was, of course, Billy Carter. Dreamed up by the since defunct Falls City Brewing Co. of Louisville, Billy Beer sales went flat not long after its much heralded introduction in 1977.

16. The Chordettes were originally sponsored by *Kingsbury* Breweries. It probably didn't hurt that one member of the quartet was the daughter of King Cole, Kingsbury's prexy.

17. The Clydesdales have been in use since 1933, the year beer came back. Before Prohibition, Anheuser-Busch had teams of oxen that toured the country for promotional purposes.

18. Mississippi. Every other state, including such unlikely candidates as Alabama, Vermont, Maine, and New Mexico, have had at least one operating brewery through the years.

19. Bob Elliott and Ray Goulding, better known as Bob and Ray, played the ever-zany Bert and Harry.

20. "It's the Water" is the slogan for Olympia Beer and has been since 1902, seven years after veteran brewer Leopold Schmidt located his brewery next to the Deschutes River in Tumwater, Washington.

The *From Beer to Eternity* Rating Scale

So, how'd you do? Here's how the official rating scale lines up:

# of Correct Answers	From Beer to Eternity Rating
18–20	Brewery President (with all the beer you want)
15–17	Brewmaster (with all the beer you can make)
11–14	Bottling Superintendent (with all the beer you can fit in your car's trunk)
6–10	Bottle Washer (with all the beer you can fit in your car's glove compartment)
1–5	Floorsweep (with all the beer you can fit in the palm of your hand)
0	You're fired!

The Bottle with the Blue Ribbon

Wanted: Women who are clean of mind, pure of heart, and facile of hand. Team spirit a plus. Track record with ribbon a must. Results-oriented self-starters only. Apply 246-BEER.

Such might have read a Milwaukee help wanted ad of a hundred years ago. The prospective employer: Pabst (or its predecessor company, the Phillip Best Brewing Co.), of course.

In 1882 the brewery decided to do a little window dressing with respect to one of its more obscure brands, a light lager called Select. Somebody said, "Why not tie a piece of blue ribbon around the neck of Select's bottles?" Somebody else said, "Why not?" And so they did.

Actually "they" didn't . . . but little old ladies (and little old men, too?) did. By hand. Yards and yards and yards of it. Thus was born one of THE great packaging ideas of all time. Almost from that moment on, Select could have been spelled "success." The bright blue ribbon did indeed dress up the bottle, making it stand out from the growing crowd of bottled beers. People found it easy to say, "Give me the bottle with the blue ribbon." Sales of Select soared. By the the early 1890s, Pabst was ordering — and using — over three hundred thousand yards of blue ribbon a year . . . real silk blue ribbon, not your imitation plastic stuff.

Still, though, there was no mention of Blue Ribbon as a brand name. It was not until 1895, thirteen years after the ribbon's

MARKED BY A DELICIOUS FLAVOR. Pabst Select as it appeared in an 1892 souvenir-of-the-brewery booklet, looking good in clear glass, decked out in blue ribbon, and described: "Marked by a delicious flavor and by highly tonic properties." It would be another three years before the words *blue ribbon* found their way onto the label.

debut, that the words *blue ribbon* were added to Select's label. Two years later, in April 1897, Blue Ribbon replaced Select as the brand's name, and in 1900 Pabst trademarked Blue Ribbon as the name for its lager.

Although the tying of a piece of actual blue ribbon has long since gone the way of most labor-intensive operations, the name — and the spirit, too — lives on. Call it Pabst Blue Ribbon, call it PBR, call it Blue . . . but call it a darned good idea way back in 1882.

> "Once, during Prohibition, I was forced to live for days on nothing but food and water."
> — *W. C. Fields*

This Sud's for You: An Interview with Fritz Maytag

When you think of Maytag what do you think of?

Suds.

When you think of Fritz Maytag — and his Anchor Brewing Co. of San Francisco — what do you think of?

Suds!

Fritz, the great-grandson of the washing machine company's founder, is proprietor, president, brewmaster, and all-around chief, cook, and bottle washer at what has rightfully become a West Coast cult brewery among beer aficionados. And rightfully is the right word because Fritz Maytag brews damn good beers. Moreover, he started doing so at a time when distinctive brews were on the verge of becoming an endangered species. *Business Week* has called Fritz Maytag "the undisputed father of micro-breweries." *From Beer to Eternity* asked Fritz what he thought about it all, from the very beginning up through right now. Here's what he had to say:

What's the real story of you and your involvement with Anchor?

The real story is that in the fifties I was a student at Stanford, and there was a bar near the campus which was one of the two or three best bars. It was called the Oasis, known as the O. Famous all over the world, with a capital "O." Not just the western world, the whole world, as the O. It was the first bar over the creek, in Menlo Park.

They had great hamburgers and lots of beer. And they often had — but not all the

time — Anchor Steam on draft. I well remember one night somebody saying, "You know, you oughtta try Anchor Steam." And I did. And it made an impression on me only that it was an interesting local beer.

When you first tried it, then, you didn't think it was distinctive or anything?

Honestly I thought it was a little odd, which it was. It wasn't a beer exactly. It was interesting. I didn't fall in love with it, but I do remember that I was told it was an interesting local phenomenon, and that made an impression on me. But the beer did not make a big impression on me.

And then in 1965, and for years before, I'd hang out at the Old Spaghetti Factory, which was this wonderful watering hole in San Francisco that was started in 1957. I knew the owner, Freddie Kuh, and he had Anchor Steam on draft. He had put Anchor Steam on draft from the moment he opened the Old Spaghetti Factory. He was the first bar in modern times to take a little, local brewery and make it part of his atmosphere, part of his whole concept for this restaurant.

Well, one night in 1965 Freddie said to me, "Have you ever been down to the brewery?" I said, "No I never have." He said, "You ought to go down there. They're going to close tomorrow or the next day. I've been trying to keep them alive, and I can't do it, and they're bankrupt. It's the second or third time in the last ten years. You really ought to go down and take a look because you like that sort of thing and it's really interesting."

So I went down. I don't remember thinking that I would buy it, but I do remember a sense of excitement. And I think I was at a point in my life when I was certainly ready for something kinda crazy, like getting involved in a brewery or something. I went down there and I met the guy who was running it, whose name was Lawrence Steese. He was an amazing character, kind of a jack of all trades: part mechanic, part artist, part poet, part wobbly. Wonderful guy; smoked a pipe. He mumbled. Just had

I DIDN'T FALL IN LOVE WITH IT. "It wasn't a beer exactly. It was interesting. I didn't fall in love with it."

GUESS WHAT I DID TODAY? "I've tried to explain to people: you go home and say, 'Guess what I did today . . . I bought a brewery.'"

a lot of atmosphere.

Anyway, he was there and they were desperate. They were literally going to close everything the next day. And he got to talking and he more or less talked me into buying it. It didn't take very long. I looked around. It was fascinating. I found out I could buy 51 percent of the stock and save it from bankruptcy the next day for almost no money: I mean, basically what you'd pay for a used car.

I called my attorney, who was a good beer drinker and a guy who'd gone to Stanford and Stanford Law School and had drunk many a pitcher at the O. I asked him if he'd heard of Anchor Steam and he said, "Sure." And I said, "Well great. Come up to San Francisco because I'm going to buy the brewery."

Were they still making authentic steam beer when you bought the brewery?
It depends on what you mean by an authentic steam beer. They *were* steam beer, so anything they were doing was authentic. But they were doing some things which we quickly changed, which were the result of being desperately poor.

What makes steam beer steam beer?
Nobody knows. Today it's steam beer be-

cause we make it. Anything we make and call steam beer is steam beer, right? I'm not being facetious. What I say is that I'm the world's expert and I don't know. I would say that once upon a time steam beer seems to have been a nickname on the West Coast that came about, probably on the part of the public and probably lasting for twenty or thirty years or so, for beers made like lager but without ice-cold temperatures. They were rapidly fermented and made in shallow fermenting pans, probably to take advantage of the cold air. And carbonated by krausening, which is a second fermentation of freshly fermented beer being added to a previously fermented batch, in a wooden barrel in those days, almost certainly.

All of this is how lager beer was made, except lager beer was made at ice-cold temperatures and aged for several months, whereas this was made, I'm sure, the way English ale is made today in simple primitive breweries. It was made and sold in about eight days, I would guess, because if you don't sell it, it spoils.

So steam beer seems to have been a lager that was sold immediately. But there really can't be such a thing because lager means "to store." It [steam beer] was an instant nonlagered lager, if you will: a bottom-fermented, carbonated beer.

You, bought the brewery on a lark. Did you ever think you'd be in the beer business?
Not for one moment prior to that, no. But I must say that one moment after I bought the brewery I knew I was in the beer business. It was a thrilling idea. I've tried to explain to people: you go home and say, "Guess what I did today . . . I bought a brewery."

You're the great-grandson of the founder of the Maytag Washing Machine Company of Newton, Iowa, aren't you?
Yes, the great-grandson. His name was F. L. Maytag, the same name as mine—Frederick Lewis.

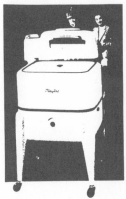

WILDEST DREAMS. "I never in my wildest dreams thought of going to work in the Maytag Company."

Continued on next page

141

SIX FANTASTIC BEERS. "I don't think there's another brewery anywhere in the world that makes such a variety of utterly distinctive and distinguished beers. I really don't. I challenge anybody. Six fantastic beers!"
— Fritz Maytag, March 1986

You, I gather, had no great desire to go back to Iowa and the washing machine business?
I never dreamed of going to work in that company. I worked there in the summers as a boy and I was very proud of it, but I never in my wildest dreams thought of going to work in the Maytag Company. My father was president, and he was an amazing, wonderful man. In the fifties never in my wildest dreams did it occur to me that he wouldn't be running the company all of his life . . . a good part of my life. Why would I want to go there? Besides, I wanted to go to California. I wanted to get out and see new things and do things on my own. I was always encouraged to do anything . . . just do something, you know.

Can you recall any humorous stories or anecdotes from back when you first took over the brewery?
Well, I don't know how humorous it was, but in the early days we'd sometimes get complaints. The no-name bar would call and say, "Gee, your dark beer doesn't seem as dark as it used to be." So we'd solve that by just adding a little more caramel coloring. You see, when I took over, that's all they'd do to make our dark beer . . . add caramel coloring. It was one of the things they were

doing to help stay alive. So I discontinued all of that, but I dreamed of the day that we could start making a real dark beer, with real dark malts.

And I can recall how hard it was in those first years to get the city of San Francisco to know that we were still around. No one knew the brewery was still there. There was no magic, no romance, no love of our brewery, no knowledge of our brewery. Nothing. No concept for what Anchor was, or steam beer, or anything. *Nobody* had heard of us and those few who had heard of us thought we'd gone out of business years ago. I would walk into an account and try to sell 'em our beer and they'd look at me and say, "That brewery went out of business." And I'd say, "No it's not out of business. I own the brewery." And they'd say, "No I'm sorry. I don't know who you are, but I *know* the brewery went bankrupt."

I know that after years of slowly but surely establishing Anchor Steam as a beer of quality, your dream of a true dark beer, Anchor Porter, became a reality in 1972 and that both Liberty Ale and your Christmas Ale were born in 1975. Tell me about your two newest products, your barley wine and your wheat beer.
Well, I got the idea for a barley wine when I visited England in 1975. We first brewed it in the fall of that year and bottled it the next spring. They call it a wine, of course, as a nickname, but it's not a wine. It's a beer. It's an ale. It's a wine by nickname because it's strong.

We call ours Old Foghorn. We named it using the British tradition of a crazy name preceded by "old." We were sitting around the taproom, by the fire probably, having a beer, and somebody said, "Alright, what're we gonna call it?" I said, "Well there's Old Roger, there's Old Nick." Somebody said, "Old Frederick," and I said, "Ha ha ha, naming it for me." I said, "No way, that wouldn't be good." And then somebody said, "How about Old Foghorn?" I knew it was great the minute I heard it.

Our wheat beer is just two years old. We

first brewed it in 1984. It's kind of a light, kind of a dry beer. We're really trying to make a thirst-quenching summer beer that has a lot of integrity and interest and quality.

People say, "Well, it's kind of a light, dry beer." But taste it: it's not Schlitz; it's not Stroh's. It's Anchor Wheat Beer. It's fantastic. It's different.

I don't think there's another brewery anywhere in the world that makes such a variety of utterly distinctive and distinguished beers. I really don't. I challenge anybody. Six fantastic beers!

What do you think of the boutique or microbrewery movement?
Oh, I think it's wonderful. I think it's fantastic. And I think that some of them will succeed. Some of these little breweries, little microbreweries — many of whom are much bigger than I was not very long ago — some of them will succeed.

It's thrilling to me that these microbreweries would exist, because they're trying to make something utterly different than from what Budweiser is trying to make. Budweiser is trying to make a product that's a marvelous, inexpensive, inoffensive product to satisfy the masses. But we, and the microbreweries, are trying to make a great beer.

How would you describe yourself now . . . in terms of being a San Francisco tradition?
In the general public's eye we are now thought of as being a San Francisco tradition. And in San Francisco itself we are considered now — thank God, and after great effort and great worry — we are considered an old, reliable sort of landmark company. No Johnny-come-lately. "Just the old brewery. Oh it's always been here. It's part of the city." And believe me, twenty years ago it was always there but nobody knew·it.

One last, somewhat heavy, question: I've always felt that America owes a not inconsiderable measure of its success to the fact that, by and large, we have been and are a

THEY'D LOOK AT ME. "I would walk into an account and try to sell 'em our beer and they'd look at me and say, 'That brewery went out of business.'"

beer-drinking nation as opposed to a wine or hard liquor–drinking nation. Have you thoughts on this?
Well, I think that beer may somehow be central to the whole nature of modern industrial, democratic countries; that where you have a lot of beer drinkers, you have democracies. Of course you have all kinds of struggling to get democracies, but you really do have them. And to me beer is something you can drink all evening while you talk in a tavern and make politics. That's why the Constitution was written in a tavern, right? . . . probably drinking beer, not rum. You drink too much rum, you don't write constitutions . . . you crawl home.

I like to think that somehow, north of the line that goes across Europe dividing beer from wine, that north of that line you have democracy. I'm not sure how far you can press that, but I think it's pretty interesting.

Beer leads to relaxation and conversation and enthusiasm, of course. We sit down; we let down our hair. We have all kinds of words for that: we roll up our sleeves; we let down our hair; we talk. But we talk. We talk rationally. We argue. You know you can drink beer and argue politics. You can't drink whiskey and argue politics: somebody gets killed.

Thank you, Fritz. Your enthusiasm and love of fine beers is a credit to the U.S. brewing industry.

Thank you, Will.

PROBABLY DRINKING BEER. "That's why the Constitution was written in a tavern, right? . . . probably drinking beer, not rum. You drink too much rum, you don't write constitutions . . . you crawl home."

Not a Dry Statistic in the Bunch

Statistics are generally dry, about as appealing as a pile of sawdust.

But here's a bunch that are good and wet. After all, how can *anything* pertaining to beer be dry?! Take your time in looking over the various charts and tables. You'll be amazed at all the worthwhile — even fascinating — stuff you'll learn, impress your friends and acquaintances, too. Stumpers like "Hey Joe, I'll bet you don't know South Dakota's annual per capita brew consumption" (answer — 21.7 gallons) are bound to go over big.

Estimated Total Consumption by State, 1984
(In Hundreds of 31-Gallon Barrels)

Alabama	2,319	Missouri	3,837
Alaska	458	Montana	781
Arizona	2,939	Nebraska	1,315
Arkansas	1,357	Nevada	1,031
California	20,632	New Hampshire	1,123
Colorado	2,633	New Jersey	5,224
Connecticut	2,063	New Mexico	1,299
Delaware	526	New York	11,875
District of		North Carolina	3,931
Columbia	587	North Dakota	531
Florida	10,283	Ohio	8,630
Georgia	4,007	Oklahoma	1,892
Hawaii	961	Oregon	1,947
Idaho	748	Pennsylvania	9,573
Illinois	9,147	Rhode Island	779
Indiana	3,908	South Carolina	2,342
Iowa	2,240	South Dakota	495
Kansas	1,632	Tennessee	2,991
Kentucky	2,222	Texas	15,356
Louisiana	3,429	Utah	714
Maine	826	Vermont	450
Maryland	3,375	Virginia	4,077
Massachusetts	4,560	Washington	3,058
Michigan	6,789	West Virginia	1,238
Minnesota	3,161	Wisconsin	5,064
Mississippi	1,686	Wyoming	434

Source: The Brewing Industry in the United States, published by the U.S. Brewers Association, 1750 K Street, NW, Washington, D.C. 20006

Market Share
(Percentage of Total U.S. Beer Sales by Each of the 5 Largest Brewers)

1985

Anheuser-Busch, Inc.	37.2%
Miller Brewing Co.	20.3%
Stroh Brewery Co.	12.8%
G. Heileman Brewing Co.	8.9%
Adolph Coors Co.	8.1%
All others	12.7%
	100%

1975

Anheuser-Busch, Inc.	23%
Jos. Schlitz	15%
Pabst Brewing Co.	10%
Miller Brewing Co.	8%
Adolph Coors Co.	8%
All others	36%
	100%

1965

Anheuser-Busch, Inc.	11%
Jos. Schlitz Brewing Co.	8%
Pabst Brewing Co.	8%
Falstaff Brewing Co.	6%
Carling Brewing Co.	5%
All others	62%
	100%

Source: Modern Brewery Age Blue Book, published by Modern Brewery Age, 22 S. Smith Street, Norwalk, Conn. 06855

The only brewing company to have remained in the top five over the past two decades is A-B ... and they've done a lot more than "remain": they've become almost totally dominant.

California's way ahead in terms of total beer consumption now ... but I'd gladly bet a couple of six-packs on Texas a decade or so down the road!

These figures include all of each state's residents. Figure in just those folks twenty-one and over and the numbers rise dramatically ... to 51.7 for New Hampshire, 50.5 for Nevada, etc.

New Hampshire, Nevada, and Wisconsin just about always slug it out (slurp it out?) to see which'll be numero uno.

It would take a month of statewide beer blasts for Utah to lose its position at the bottom of the beer-drinking heap.

Moscow's been pushing beer as an alternative to vodka and other hard stuff.

World's Leading Total Beer-Production Nations, 1984
(In 31-Gallon Barrels)

United States	193,020,626
West Germany	78,645,000
Russia	56,330,000*
United Kingdom	52,384,000
Japan	39,788,000
Brazil	24,160,000
East Germany	22,157,000
Mexico	21,375,000
Czechoslovakia	20,265,000
Canada	19,611,000
Spain	18,605,000
France	17,289,000
China	17,045,000
Australia	16,148,000
The Netherlands	14,528,000
Belgium	12,783,000*

Source: The Brewing Industry in the United States, published by the U.S. Brewers Association, 1750 K Street, NW, Washington, D.C. 20006

*estimated

Per Capita Consumption by State, 1984
(In Gallons)

Alabama	18.0	Missouri	23.7
Alaska	28.4	Montana	29.4
Arizona	29.8	Nebraska	25.4
Arkansas	17.9	Nevada	35.1
California	25.0	New Hampshire	35.6
Colorado	25.7	New Jersey	21.5
Connecticut	20.3	New Mexico	28.3
Delaware	26.6	New York	20.8
District of		North Carolina	19.8
Columbia	29.2	North Dakota	24.0
Florida	29.0	Ohio	24.9
Georgia	21.3	Oklahoma	17.8
Hawaii	28.7	Oregon	22.6
Idaho	23.2	Pennsylvania	24.9
Illinois	24.6	Rhode Island	25.1
Indiana	22.0	South Carolina	22.0
Iowa	23.9	South Dakota	21.7
Kansas	20.7	Tennessee	19.7
Kentucky	18.5	Texas	29.8
Louisiana	23.8	Utah	13.4
Maine	22.1	Vermont	26.3
Maryland	24.1	Virginia	22.4
Massachusetts	24.4	Washington	21.8
Michigan	23.2	West Virginia	19.7
Minnesota	23.5	Wisconsin	32.9
Mississippi	20.1	Wyoming	26.3
Total U.S. Average			23.9

Source: The Brewing Industry in the United States, published by the U.S. Brewers Association, 1750 K Street, NW, Washington, D.C. 20006

The United States is first ... and by a wide margin.

Add together the two Germanies and you top the one hundred million barrel mark ... remarkable for such a relatively small country.

Not a Dry Statistic in the Bunch, Continued

Top five metros account for total U.S. 14.3 percent of total U.S. beer business; top fifteen, beer business; top 25.7 percent; top twenty-five, 34.5 percent.

We may rank but twelfth among the world's nations, but our per capita has increased dramatically in the past fifty years.

Top 25 Metro Areas in Total Beer Sales, 1984

	Metro Area	Millions of Barrels	% of U.S. Total
1	Los Angeles/ Long Branch	7,271	4.0
2	New York City	6,514	3.6
3	Chicago	4,990	2.7
4	Philadelphia	3,829	2.1
5	Detroit	3,406	1.9
6	Boston/Lawrence/ Salem/Lowell/ Brockton	2,888	1.6
7	Houston	2,655	1.4
8	Washington, D.C.	2,349	1.3
9	Dallas	2,132	1.2
10	Nassau/Suffolk	1,875	1.0
11	Pittsburgh	1,856	1.0
12	Baltimore	1,805	1.0
13	Anaheim/ Santa Ana	1,794	1.0
14	Miami/Hialeah	1,733	1.0
15	Tampa/ St. Petersburg/ Clearwater	1,708	1.0
16	Cleveland	1,689	0.9
17	San Diego	1,679	0.9
18	Milwaukee	1,666	0.9
19	Minneapolis/ St. Paul	1,651	0.9
20	San Francisco	1,644	0.9
21	St. Louis	1,644	0.9
22	Phoenix	1,623	0.9
23	Oakland	1,554	0.8
24	Denver	1,362	0.8
25	Atlanta	1,309	0.7

Source: Modern Brewery Age Blue Book, published by Modern Brewery Age, 22 S. Smith Street, Norwalk, Conn. 06855

1985 Sales of the Biggies — America's Ten Largest Brewing Companies
(In 31-Gallon Barrels)

1	Anheuser-Busch, Inc.	68,000,000
2	Miller Brewing Co.	37,100,000
3	Stroh Brewery Co.	23,400,000
4	G. Heileman Brewing Co.	16,200,000
5	Adolph Coors Co.	14,738,000
6	Pabst Brewing Co.	8,900,000*
7	Genesee Brewing Co.	3,000,000
8	Christian Schmidt	2,100,000*
9	Falstaff Brewing Co. (including Pearl and General Brewing Cos.)	1,998,458
10	Pittsburgh Brewing Co.	857,547

*Estimated

Source: Modern Brewery Age Blue Book, published by Modern Brewery Age, 22 S. Smith Street, Norwalk, Conn. 06855

United States Beer Production
(In 31-Gallon Barrels)

1905	49,522,029	1950	88,807,075
1910	59,552,229	1955	89,791,154
1915	59,808,210	1960	94,547,867
1919	27,712,648	1965	108,015,217
1933	11,059,071	1970	134,653,881
1935	45,228,605	1975	157,870,017
1940	54,891,737	1980	188,373,657
1945	86,604,080	1985	193,794,790

United States Per Capita Beer Consumption
(In Gallons)

1935	10.3	1965	16.0
1940	12.5	1970	18.7
1945	18.6	1975	21.1
1950	17.2	1980	23.1
1955	15.9	1984	23.9
1960	15.4		

Source: The Brewing Industry in the United States, published by the U.S. Brewers Association, 1750 K Street, NW, Washington, D.C.

Sex: 59 percent of all American males 18 and over can be classified as beer drinkers, versus 37 percent percent of like-aged females.

Age: All age ranges hold their own when it comes to drinking beer, but the age range that upholds it the most is the 18-24 year old group, followed closely (so closely it's a virtual tie) by the 25-34 group.

Worldwide Biggies
World's Ten Largest Brewing Companies
1984 Sales Estimates
(*In 31-Gallon Barrels*)

1	Anheuser-Busch, Inc. (U.S.)	64,000,000
2	Miller Brewing Co. (U.S.)	37,500,000
3	Heineken N.V. (The Netherlands)	29,400,000
4	Kiren Brewery Co., Ltd. (Japan)	24,527,000
5	Stroh Brewery Co. (U.S.)	23,900,000
6	G. Heileman Brewing Co. (U.S.)	16,760,000
7	Companhia Cervejaria Brahma (Brazil)	16,200,000
8	Kronenbourg (France)	15,750,000
9	Adolph Coors Co. (U.S.)	13,187,000
10	United Breweries (Carlsberg) (Denmark)	11,931,000

Source: Modern Brewery Age Blue Book, published by Modern Brewery Age, 22 S. Smith Street, Norwalk, Conn. 06855

World's Leading Per Capita Beer
Consumption Nations, 1981
(In Litres)

West Germany	147.0
East Germany	141.4
Czechoslovakia	140.1
Australia	134.1
Denmark	131.0
Belgium	124.0
Luxembourg	118.6
New Zealand	117.7
Ireland	116.4
United Kingdom	111.5
Austria	104.8
United States	93.3
The Netherlands	89.6
Canada	86.4

Source: The Brewers' Society International Statistical Handbook

So Who Drinks Beer?!

By special permission of New York's Simmons Market Research Bureau, Inc., we're going to close with perhaps the "wettest" of all beer drinking statistics, a profile of America's beer drinkers . . . all 80,301,000 of them (of us!).

Drinkers of Any Beer

	# Drinkers (000)	% Composition	% Incidence
Total Adults (18+)	80,301	100.0%	47.4%
Males	47,200	59.8	59.0
Females	33,100	41.2	37.0
18–24	15,953	19.9	55.8
25–34	22,323	27.8	55.7
35–44	15,226	19.0	50.5
45–54	10,229	12.7	45.8
55–64	8,713	10.9	39.6
65+	7,858	9.8	29.8
Graduated College	15,797	19.7	55.1
Attended College	15,550	19.4	52.3
Graduated High School	31,942	39.8	47.5
Did not Graduate High School	17,012	21.2	38.9
Professional/ Manager	15,200	18.9	57.4
Tech/Clerical/Sales	16,214	20.2	51.2
Precision/Craft	7,530	9.4	58.6
Other Employed	16,397	20.4	52.8
Not Employed	24,961	31.1	37.0

Source: © Simmons Market Research Bureau: 1985 Study of Media and Markets

Education: You don't have to be smart to enjoy beer, but it helps. The more education, the higher the percentage of beer drinkers . . . ranging from 55.1 percent for college grads to 38.9 percent for high school dropouts.

Occupation: As with education, it seems the higher the job, the greater the percentage of beer drinkers. One thing's for certain: regardless of level, it helps to be employed to be a beer drinker . . . but then again, there aren't too many places giving away free beer anymore.

Mr. Budman

THE BUDMAN'S GREATEST TRIUMPH. Ed Nichols standing tall in front of his favorite piece, a recently acquired 1903 "Budweiser's Greatest Triumph" lithograph.

How does one earn the title "Budman"? By drinking a lot of Budweiser? By collecting Bud memorabilia? By doing a king-sized job of both? To find out we traveled deep into the heart of the Flatbush section of Brooklyn and talked with the Budman himself, Ed Nichols.

I understand they call you the Budman. Is that true, Ed?
That's me, the Budman. Been that way for at least fifteen years now.

How'd you pick up the name?
Actually it was given to me by my present wife, Rose Ann—at the time she was my girlfriend—'cause I drank so much Budweiser and I started picking up all this Budweiser stuff. She called me the Budman. So I applied for a license plate . . . and since then I've been the Budman.

How many years have you had the Budman plate?
Seven years now. Before that it was Bud 210, which is my date of birth, February 10, 1938.

What is—and has been—your fascination with Budweiser?
Well, I've always been a beer drinker, just like yourself and most guys we know. Actu-

ally, I've had more Piel's, Schaefer, and Rheingold things in my original collection than I did anything else. But being that I drank so much Budweiser, people started bringing me Budweiser items—trays, shirts, old mugs they found in their basement. From there to flea markets to breweriana sales, it became just strictly Anheuser-Busch. That was 1976. As a matter of fact, it was during Budweiser's centennial.

What has made you always drink Budweiser?
Actually that's really a falsehood. I don't always drink Budweiser. I'll drink any beer on the market that's a good beer. I drink Budweiser because I like Budweiser. To me it always tastes the same. But I'll drink Stroh's, Straub, any beer that's good. The only beer I won't drink is Miller. And the only reason is because it's a cigarette company.

Your whole basement—as I'm sitting here— is filled with almost nothing but Anheuser-Busch and Budweiser stuff. Is this your pride and joy?
Oh, absolutely. I spend 99 percent of my life here. I'm constantly moving things, redesigning, rebuilding. I just love it. It's always a new challenge; there's always something else to find. I amaze myself sometimes!

What's your proudest moment been in your years of collecting?
My proudest moment is probably right now. I'm serious. It's being recognized by another member of the fraternity of collecting, of people that appreciate things. It's a recognition that I guess everybody more or less looks for. I don't expect to be on front-page news, but it's nice to be recognized as a serious person and not just a goof-off that collects 1985 plastic signs.

That's right, you collect new as well as old stuff.
I used to. But now I think the newest I have in my collection is probably 1975. And I'm more or less backing off. I'm going back into the past. As I gain older stuff I get rid of the newer stuff.

What makes you collect?
I collect for the enjoyment of it . . . same reason anybody collects stamps, coins, or whatever they collect. I collect for the absolute enjoyment of having something that I enjoy looking at, showing to other people. And believe it or not, this place can be a regular subway station, with people comin' in and out to see the collection. That's my third guest book. I'd say untold hundreds and hundreds of people have been through this collection. From all over the East Coast. I've had half the New York City police department and fire department down here. I've had the fire department down here on call [on duty]. It was New Years Eve, 1985. Three of my friends called the fire department and said there was a water leak just so the firemen could see the collection.

One last question, Ed. Have you been to St. Louis and, if so, how did you feel about Anheuser-Busch's brewery and headquarters and everything?
I was in awe. I couldn't use any other term but to say I was in awe. It was like going to your old homeland. To me it was just beautiful . . . the old buildings, the old brewery. Everything was just beautiful. It was one of the moments that I really enjoyed in my life. I had planned spending three days there; I spent two weeks.

FUN. The Budman and his Budmobile. Ed sums up his years of collecting Bud memorabilia in one fun-filled sentence: "It's been fun; it will be fun; it'll always be fun."

The Mystery of the "33"

Rolling Rock. It's often referred to as "the Coors of the East." (Or is Coors the Rolling Rock of the West?!) It has that same light, mellow flavor, that same mystique. And it's a mystique punctuated all the more by the mysterious "33" that appears on the reverse side of every Rolling Rock bottle's paper label (and on the bottle cap, too).

Up until now no one's been quite sure what the numbers mean or why they're there, and for good reason . . . no one really *does* know what they mean or why they're there.

The generally accepted answer is that the "33" is short for 1933, the year Prohibition ended and the Latrobe Brewing Co., brewers of Rolling Rock, started back in operation. However, the folks at the brewery, located in Latrobe, Pennsylvania, point out that Rolling Rock's now semilegendary painted label bottle design includes exactly 33 words permanently printed on the back of the bottle, and that there are exactly 33 letters in the listing of their all-natural ingredients. And Rock aficionados have been known to boast the twin threes are there because Rolling Rock is 33 times better tasting than that other beer that comes in a green bottle.

So take your pick and while you're taking it, try saying Rolling Rock 33 times in a row. Out loud. Quickly. Get it down pat and it's guaranteed to make you the life of the party. Guaranteed.

THIS IS A BEER THAT'S EVERYTHING A FINE IMPORTED BEER OUGHT TO BE. "33"

ROLLING ROCK PREMIUM BEER IMPORTED FROM LATROBE, PA.

"IMPORTED FROM LATROBE, PA." Through the years there've been three different breweries in Latrobe, a smallish city about 25 miles southeast of Pittsburgh, but the only one that's hung in there is the Latrobe Brewing Co., still going strong as it approaches one hundred (it started rolling out the barrels in 1893). (Courtesy Latrobe Brewing Co.)

Have a Healthy

I'm not going to sit here and say that drinking beer will make you healthy, wealthy, and wise or that it'll triple your sex life; but *consumed in moderation*, beer is a beverage that has almost invariably been viewed as good for both body and mind.

The ancients drank beer to renew both their physical and spiritual strength. The Egyptians especially knew its value in health: a good one hundred of their standard prescriptions contained beer.

German doctors have long, long prescribed beer. In days of old, many used it to enrich the blood. Many more subscribed to the time-honored German saying "*Die Brauerei ist die beste Apotheke*"—the brewery is the best pharmacy.

In the 1600s French doctors prescribed beer for a whole range of maladies from cancer to typhoid fever, with diabetes, grippe, and smallpox in between.

Although beer obviously didn't cure diabetes, smallpox, or anything else, it was probably as good or better a prescription as other remedies used in those days. At least it was relatively safe to drink (as opposed to water or milk, both of which often contained all sorts of impurities), possessed a goodly assortment of vitamins and minerals, and, if nothing else, eased the patient's tension.... which often went a long way in curing whatever it was that was ailing.

"NATURE'S TONIC FOR WEARY HEADS AND HANDS." A bevy of pre-Prohibition "Beer is Pure, Beer is Healthy" ads. C. H. Evans & Sons, a long-respected Hudson, New York, British-tradition brewer, was especially wont to promote the health benefits of its Evans Ale. Their product was good ... and so was their copy.

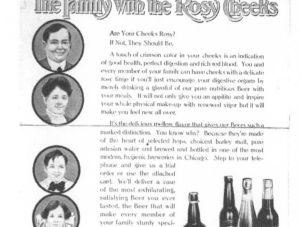

"THE FAMILY WITH THE ROSY CHEEKS." Circa 1910 promotional piece from Chicago's Wacker & Birk Brewing Co. touting beer—Wacker & Birk Beer, anyway—as a drink for the entire family. Such a suggestion would undoubtedly incur the wrath of the multitudes today.

It's this latter quality — its relaxing properties — that has long led the medical fraternity to recommend beer to their high-strung, anemic, or otherwise weak patients. Beer relaxes the system so the patient is better able to properly ingest necessary nutrients. Plus beer contains, as mentioned above, a host of goodies itself. The brewing process leaves about 65 percent of the original grain nutritional value. A twelve-ounce bottle or can of beer empties twelve grams of carbohydrates plus healthy doses of protein, thiamin, riboflavin, magnesium, calcium, phosphorus, and potassium into the system.

In the late 1950s (1958 to be exact), the American Medical Association reported research conducted by Noah D. Fabrican, a Chicago otolaryngologist (ear and throat specialist), that indicated beer might be helpful in fighting the common cold.

More recent studies, in the 1970s and 1980s, strongly indicate that beer — once again, consumed in moderation — might well be an effective heart attack preventative. Men who drank one or two bottles or cans of beer a day had almost half the heart attack rate of men who were nondrinkers. Scientists aren't quite sure why this is so, but the thought is that beer's alcohol increases the type of cholesterol that's good (HDL — high-density lipoprotein) in the bloodstream. This, in turn, has a definite positive effect against coronary artery disease.

In a March 1986 interview in San Francisco, two-time Nobel Prize winner and noted health buff Linus Pauling outlined his "Pauling's 12 Steps to Health" program. One of them — you guessed it — is to enjoy alcohol. And to enjoy it in the only right way . . . in moderation.

Right on, Dr. Pauling!

TELL IT LIKE IT IS. "City Water Is Not Fit to Drink! USE GERMAN BEER!" reads this December 1910 ad from Cumberland, Maryland's German Brewing Company.

Times haven't changed a whole awful lot. In areas where water's purity is suspect (Mexico comes readily to mind), beer is still your safest bet. (Courtesy Allegany County Historical Society, Inc. Cumberland, Maryland)

License plate, Park Slope, Brooklyn, May 1986

BEER DRINKERS MAKE BETTER LOVERS.
Do beer drinkers really make better lovers?
Is the Pope Catholic?
Does a bear sit in the woods?
Of course, beer drinkers make better lovers. The only problem is that proof positive of this fact is hard to come by.
Which means, of course, that you'll just have to go on out and prove it for yourself!

Where in These Sudsy United States Are You?

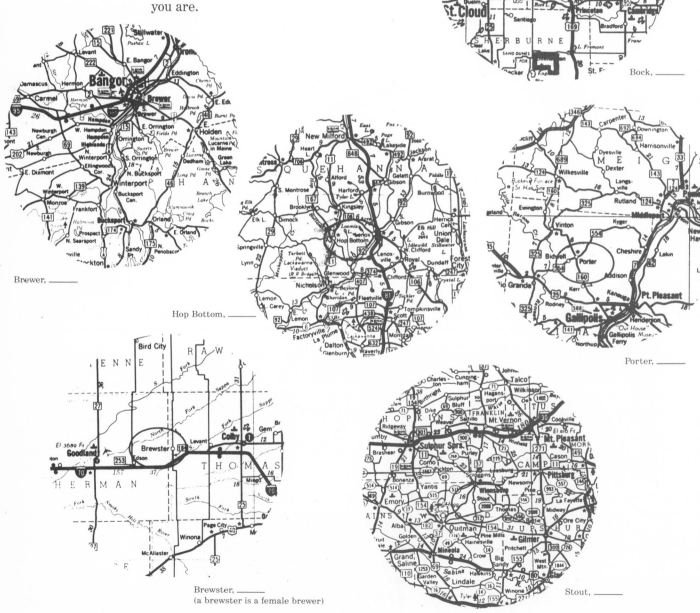

Here's a page tailor-made for all you American geography buffs out there. The idea: to tell what state you're in when you're in each of the following "beer towns."

You'll have to be good. A few of the towns are easy, but a few are real toughies.

Bon beer voyage. And don't forget to send postcards . . . once you figure out where you are.

Bock, _____

Brewer, _____

Hop Bottom, _____

Porter, _____

Brewster, _____
(a brewster is a female brewer)

Stout, _____

Maps courtesy TravelVision Maps © General Drafting Company, Inc.

152

On Loaning Money in St. Louis . . .
or How Budweiser Came to Be

Who loans what to whom in St. Louis or any other place hardly sounds as if it were a candidate for "The Most Stimulating Topic of the Year Award" . . . but if it hadn't been for a series of loans in the Queen City of the Mississippi over a century ago, it's quite safe to say that today's beer picture in America would be very different than it is. And it's a definite to say that this Bud would not be for you.

Here's how it all went, starting back in 1857. Four years before the start of the Civil War, the small Bavarian Brewery on Pestalozzi Street in St. Louis, of course, went bankrupt. Eberhard Anheuser, a German immigrant who'd made considerable money as a St. Louis soap manufacturer, had loaned the brewery ninety thousand dollars. When the brewery went under, Anheuser assumed control of it.

Enter Adolphus Busch. Born into a wealthy family in Germany, Busch was the youngest of twenty-one children, and he decided to come to America to seek his fortune. He arrived in St. Louis in 1857, the same year Anheuser took over the Bavarian Brewery.

Within two years Adolphus Busch owned a brewer's supply store and Eberhard Anheuser, who had not been able to turn the brewery around, was in debt to Busch for brewing materials purchased on credit. The debt was cancelled in a novel way. Adolphus was courting Lilly Eberhard, one of Eberhard's four daughters. One month before the Civil War broke out they were married. By 1863 Busch was part owner of the brewery; by 1873 he was a full partner.

Now it's Budweiser time. In 1876 Adolphus Busch met Carl Conrad, a St. Louis wine dealer recently returned from a trip through Bohemia (now a part of Czechoslovakia). While there, he lunched one day in the small city of Budweis, on the banks of the Vltava River. Wine dealer or not, Conrad liked a brew or two with lunch. The monks in the local monastery brewed the local favorite. Conrad tried it and loved it. So impressed was he, in fact, that he made a beeline for the monastery, where he suc-ceeded in obtaining the beer's formula and right to brew it in the United States. Conrad named his beer Budweiser.

Back home in St. Louis, Conrad con-tracted with Busch to brew Budweiser for him and it sold well. In 1880, however, some of Conrad's other business ventures went sour, and Busch loaned him money to stay afloat.

That same year Eberhard Anheuser passed away, leaving Busch in full control. Anxious to expand the business, Busch liked what he saw when he saw Budweiser. He decided to try to buy the American rights to it from Conrad. He offered Conrad the elimination of the debt, a substantial amount of additional money, and an executive job at the brewery. It was a most generous offer. Conrad accepted.

Busch was now free to roll . . . and roll he did. He noticed what Conrad had noticed earlier: Budweiser had unique properties that allowed it to keep well when bottled, and it could be pasteurized, further retard-ing spoilage, with the loss of virtually none of its flavor. Mr. B decided to go for broke with respect to Budweiser. He decided to forget the local market and instead take Budweiser — in bottles — national.

It was a bold move, indeed; but history has certainly recorded it as a most suc-cessful one. Today Budweiser is the largest selling beer in the world. One can only wonder how different it all would have been if credit hadn't been given so freely in St. Louis five score and more years ago.

EBERHARD ANHEUSER. He started the series of loans that started it all.

"ORIGINAL BUDWEISER LAGER BIER". A calling card from the late 1870s, when Carl Conrad was sole proprietor for "Origi-nal Budweiser Lager Bier." Carl was not to enjoy such status for long.

153

There Is No Wisdom as Wise as a Wise Brewer's Wisdom

Louis F. Neuweiler
1848–1929

Actually Louis F. Neuweiler, looking here as if he'd just swallowed some of those bad oats, was a wise brewer... and a good one. And so were the several generations of Neuweilers that followed him. They produced an outstanding line of beers, ales, and porter from 1891 until the brewery's closing in 1968. Their cream ale was held in especially high esteem all along the mid-Atlantic seaboard and was the feature of the house at McGillen's Old Ale House, long a favorite haunt of Philadelphia beer mavens.

It has been said: "There is no wisdom as wise as a wise brewer's wisdom," and with that we cannot disagree. Here, almost as if to prove the point, are a number of adages (wisdom-isms?) in a series put out around 1950 by the Louis F. Neuweiler's Sons Brewery of Allentown, Pennsylvania, in the form of business cards. They are presented here in the form of — what else — a Wheel of Wisdom.

Impress Your Friends

It's easy to visualize these cards being passed back and forth among friends and co-workers or, when feeling wild and crazy, slipped to a stranger in the supermarket or while waiting for a red light to change. And can you imagine the wonderful reaction they'd get in the New York City subway system?!

NEUWEILER'S LIGHT LAGER BEER. Their beer may have been light, but their wisdom wasn't.

154

Twinkle, Twinkle

NEUWEILER'S CREAM ALE. Described as having "natural tang and zestful flavor."

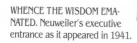

WHENCE THE WISDOM EMANATED. Neuweiler's executive entrance as it appeared in 1941.

The Star of David — or Mogen David — is usually thought to connote a temple or synagogue, but many brewmasters ago it also had a second meaning. Brewers used it to signify that a fresh batch had been brewed and was ready for serving (translation: drinking). As brewing technology improved, fresh batches were ready all year long, and the star evolved into standing for just plain freshness. As such it was used into the early part of this century. Look for it on early beer advertising.

LATE BEER ADVERTISING, TOO. What certainly appears to be a Star of David is still in use today by the Cold Spring Brewing Co., Cold Spring, Minnesota, for its highly respected Cold Spring Export.

GET IT WHILE IT'S FRESH. The brew crew at Wilkes-Barre, Pennsylvania's Stegmaier Brewing Company was more than ready and willing to taste-test the new batch — signified by the star on the barrel — in this circa 1890 view.

The Largest Restaurant of Them All

FREDERICK PABST. He had visions of New York grandeur.

CALLING ALL POTENTATES. You'd feel right at home — just you and 1,399 other folks — at Pabst Harlem. (Photo courtesy Gary Nowlin)

Interior PABST HARLEM New York

All those who know where the largest restaurant in America is, raise your hand.

My hand is not raised. I have no idea where the largest restaurant in America is. Probably somewhere in Texas.

Ah, but if you asked me about when the largest restaurant in America was owned by a brewery . . . well, that's another story.

It was in Harlem. One hundred twenty-fifth Street near Eighth Avenue . . . when Harlem was basically a white, middle-class section of New York City, a section on the rise. The restaurant was the Pabst Harlem, and it opened in September 1900 with a seating capacity of 1,400 — the largest restaurant in America.

The Pabst Harlem was more than a restaurant, however; it was part of Frederick Pabst's marketing plan to crack the New York beer market. In those days, before Prohibition, brewers were allowed to control their own outlets. Called "tied houses," only the brewer's own beer was sold.

New York City's brewers, especially George Ehret, had used such tied houses to gain a tight grip on the city's saloon sales. The only way for Pabst to make a splash was for him, figuratively speaking, to build his own pool. And that's exactly what he did, except that what he built was more like his own ocean.

Pabst's first move was to construct the Pabst Hotel on Forty-second Street at Broadway, right in the heart of today's Times Square. Opened in 1899 with a then-awesome nine stories, it was one of New York's first skyscrapers. It was also the ultimate bachelor pad. Although women were allowed into their own special glass-enclosed dining room on the second floor, only unmarried men were permitted to rent a room. Pabst also opened a large restaurant and theater just off Columbus Circle, the Pabst Grand Circle Restaurant. And in Coney Island, Pabst's Loop, a mammoth pavilion, dispensed Blue Ribbon to throngs of thirsty merrymakers.

But it was Pabst Harlem that was far and away the crowning achievement of them all. At the time it was felt that the city's upper, upper West Side could well develop into the most fashionable area of the Big Apple. Consequently, no expense was spread to make Pabst Harlem not only the largest but also the grandest eating establishment in the country. Here's how it was described in the April 15, 1906, Sunday edition of the *Milwaukee Sentinel*:

No finer restaurant of its kind than "Pabst Harlem" at 125th Street, New York, can be found in America. At great cost it was built to please the residents of this thriving street in the aristocratic section of the metropolis and from the crowds that frequent it the owners judge themselves to have been eminently successful in their undertaking. Costly and splendid in architecture and illumination, possessing an orchestra that is only excelled in the best theatres, its 1400 seats are crowded from year's end to year's end.

"Pabst Harlem" was erected at a cost of nearly $500,000. Its exterior is on a par with other public buildings in this famous upper end of New York. Its interior is resplendent with frescoes, paintings, marble columns, colored lights, and exquisite table appointments such as might make any Old World potentate feel at home.

Ironically, for all its size and razzle-dazzle, very little is known about the life and death of the Pabst Harlem. It appears, however, to have gone out of business sometime before 1910.

Keeping Up with All That's Happening in Brew and Breweriana

There's much more going on in the world of beer and breweriana than meets the average eye. Hopefully *From Beer to Eternity* will increase your thirst ... not just for a cold one, but for further input and information about the industry and/or the hobby, too. If so, here goes:

Collecting Clubs/Associations

American Breweriana Association (ABA)
P.O. Box 6082
Colorado Springs, Colo. 80934
Cost: $20.00 annual dues
Publication: *American Breweriana Journal*

American Homebrewers Association (AHA)
P.O. Box 287
Boulder, Colo. 80306
Cost: $12.00 annual dues
Publication: *zymurgy*

Bar Tourists of America (BTA)
c/o Jack McDougall, Editor
12 Sylvester Street
Cranford, N.J. 07016
Cost: $6.00 annual dues
Publication: *Bar Tourists of America Newsletter*

Beer Can Collectors of America (BCCA)
747 Merus Court
Fenton, Mo.
Cost: $10.00 annual dues
Publication: *Beer Can Collectors News Report*

Beer Drinkers International (BDI)
P.O. Box 8536
Calabasas, Calif. 91302
Cost: $12.97 annual dues
Publication: *Suds 'N' Stuff*

Eastern Coast Breweriana Association (ECBA)
c/o Eugene P. Fink
2010 N. Broad Street
Lansdale, Pa 19446
Cost: $10.00 initiation fee;
$15.00 annual dues
Publication: *ECBA Newsletter*

National Association of Breweriana Advertising (NABA)
c/o Robert E. Jaeger
2343 Met-to-Wee Lane
Wauwatosa, Wis. 53226
Cost: $15.00 annual dues
Publication: *The Breweriana Collector*

Stein Collectors International
c/o Jack Lowenstein, Editor
P.O. Box 463
Kingston, N.J. 08528
Cost: $20.00 annual dues
Publication: *Prosit*

Magazines/Periodicals/Newsletters

All About Beer
P.O. Box 15690
Santa Ana, Calif. 92705
Cost: $19.95 yearly subscription

Amateur Brewer
Box 713
Hayward, Calif. 94543
Cost: $13.50 yearly subscription

American Breweriana Journal
see ABA above

American Can Collector
c/o Jim Hunter, Publisher
P.O. Box 291
Anderson, Ind. 46015
Cost: $15.00 yearly subscription

Bar Tourists of America Newsletter
see BTA above

Beer Can Collectors News Report
see BCCA above

Beer Marketer's Insights
c/o Jerry Steinman, editor
55 Virginia Avenue
West Nyack, N.Y. 10994
Cost: $165.00 yearly subscription

The Breweriana Collector
see NABA above

ECBA Newsletter
see ECBA above

Just for Openers
c/o Ed Kaye, editor
968 Greenwood Court
Sanibel, Fla. 33957
Cost: $12.00 yearly subscription

Modern Brewery Age
22 South Smith Street
Norwalk, Conn. 06855
Cost: $65.00 yearly subscription

Prosit
see SCI above

Suds 'N' Stuff
see BDI above

zymurgy
see AHA above

Books

There are, it's delightful to report, numerous fine books about beer and breweriana. In fact there are too many to list them all here. For the most complete and up-to-date titles available, write to:

Don Bull
Bullworks
20 Fairway Drive
Stamford, Conn. 06903

Can World
Ridgecrest Drive
Goodlettsville, Tenn. 37072

HAPPY READING!

Here a Brewery, There a Brewery

I n the spring/summer of every year, the Bureau of Alcohol, Tobacco and Firearms, division of the Department of the Treasury, issues its report ATF P 5100.13, *Breweries Authorized to Operate*. Following is the listing as published in April 1986. It's listed here exactly as contained in the report (i.e., sans zip codes even though it is a government report). The list is all-inclusive and, living up to its title, does indeed list all breweries authorized to operate. This does not necessarily mean, however, that all of these facilities are still brewing or, in fact, that they all ever did. It merely means that they were all *authorized* to do so at the time the information was compiled in early 1986.

Arizona
G. Heileman Brewing Co., Inc.
150 S. 12th St.
Phoenix

Breweries come in all sizes and shapes. Here's a glimpse at two extremes. On the left is the world's largest single brewing plant, Adolph Coors's monster facility in Golden, Colorado. Its annual capacity: fifteen million barrels. On the right is the Widmer Brewing Company's miniscule-by-comparison brewery in Portland, Oregon. Characterized by Rob Widmer, Widmer's president, as "very modest . . . not a good representative of the beer that emerges from it." Widmer's annual capacity is in the range of thirty-five hundred barrels.

Arkansas
Arkansas Brewing Co., Inc.
2307 Cantrell Road
Little Rock

California
Anchor Brewing Co.
1705 Mariposa St.
San Francisco

Anheuser-Busch, Inc.
3101 Busch Drive
Fairfield

Anheuser-Busch, Inc.
P.O. Box 2113
Los Angeles

Buffalo Bill's Brewery
1082 B Street
Hayward

Golden Pacific Brewing Co.
5515 Doyle, No. 4
Emeryville

Koryo Winery Co. (Sake Brewery)
366 W. 131 St.
Los Angeles

Koryo Winery Co.
1249 West 132nd Street
Gardena

Mendocino Brewing Co.
P.O. Box 400
Hopland

Miller Brewing Co.
15801 East First St.
Irwindale

Old Los Angeles Brewery
600 Moulton Avenue, Unit 103
Los Angeles

Ozeki San Benito
249 Hillcrest Rd.
Hollister

Palo Alto Brewing Co.
270 Santa Monica Avenue
Menlo Park

Redwood Brewing Company
21 Washington Street
Petaluma

Roaring Rock Brewery
2171 Shattuck Avenue
Berkeley

The Saxton Brewery
P.O. Box 4337
Chico

Sierra Nevada Brewing Co.
2539 Gilman Way
Chico

Stanislaus Brewing Co., Inc.
3454 Shoemake Avenue
Modesto

The Stroh Brewery Company
7521 Woodman Ave.
Los Angeles

Takara Sake USA, Inc.
708 Addison Street
Berkeley

Thousand Oaks Brewing Co.
444 Vassar Avenue
Berkeley

Truckee Brewing Company
11401 Donner Pass Road
Truckee

UC at Davis (Exp-Brewery)
Cruess Hall
Davis

Under the Oaks Brewery
415 E. Villanova Road
Ojai

Colorado
Adolph Coors Co.
Golden

Boulder Brewing Co.
2880 Wilderness Place
Boulder

Florida
Anheuser-Busch, Inc.
111 Busch Drive
Jacksonville

Anheuser-Busch, Inc.
3000 August A. Busch, Jr. Blvd.
Sulphur Springs Station
Tampa

The Florida Brewery, Inc.
202 Gandy Road
Auburndale

Pabst Brewing Co.
11111–30th Street
Tampa

Georgia
Miller Brewing Co.
405 Cordele Road
Albany

G. Heileman Brewing Co., Inc.
Ga. Highway 247 Spur
Perry

Hawaii
Honolulu Sake Brewery
  & Ice Co., Ltd.
P.O. Box 1266
Honolulu

Idaho
Snake River Brewing Co., Inc.
Route 5, Box 30A
Caldwell

Illinois
G. Heileman Brewing Co., Inc.
1201 West "E" Street
Belleville

Tae Hwa Brewing Co., Inc.
1138 Greenfield
Waukegan

Indiana
Falstaff Brewing Corp.
1019-1051 Grant Avenue
Fort Wayne

G. Heileman Brewing Co.
  of Indiana, Inc.
1301 W. Pennsylvania Street
Evansville

Iowa
Dubuque Star Brewing Co.
East 4th Street Extension
Dubuque

Millstream Brewing Company
P.O. Box 283
Amana

Louisiana
Dixie Brewing Co., Inc.
2537 Tulane Avenue
New Orleans

Maryland
G. Heileman Brewing Company, Inc.
4501 Hollins Ferry Road
Baltimore

Michigan
G. Heileman Brewing Co., Inc.
926 S. Main Street
Frankenmuth

Geyer Bros. Brewing Co.
415 South Main Street
Frankenmuth

Kalamazoo Brewing Co., Inc.
315 E. Kalamazoo Avenue
Kalamazoo

The Real Ale Company, Inc.
320 N. Main Street
Chelsea

The Stroh Brewery Co.
100 River Place
Detroit

Minnesota
Cold Spring Brewing Co.
219 North Red River Avenue
Cold Spring

G. Heileman Brewing Co., Inc.
882 W. 7th Street
St. Paul

The Stroh Brewery Co.
707 E. Minnehaha Ave.
St. Paul

August Schell Brewing Co.
South Payne St.
Outlet #400
New Ulm

Missouri
Anheuser-Busch, Inc.
One Busch Place
St. Louis

Montana
Montana Beverages Ltd.
1439 Harris Street
Helena

Continued on next page

New Hampshire
Anheuser-Busch, Inc.
1000 Daniel Webster Highway
Merrimack

New Jersey
Anheuser-Busch, Inc.
200 U.S. Highway 1
Newark

Champale, Inc.
Lalor & Lamberton Sts.
Trenton

Eastern Brewing Corp.
334 N. Washington St.
Hammonton

Pabst Brewing Co.
400 Grove Street
Newark

Vernon Valley Brewery, Inc.
Route 94
Cobblestone Village
Vernon

New York
Anheuser Busch, Inc.
2885 Belgium Road
Baldwinsville

Genessee Brewing Co., Inc.
419-445 St. Paul St.
    and 14-33 Cataract Street
Rochester

Miller Brewing Co.
P.O. Box 200
Owens Road
Fulton

West End Brewing Co.
    of Utica, N.Y.
811 Edward Street
Utica

William S. Newman Brewing Co. Inc.
32 Learned Street
Albany

North Carolina
Miller Brewing Co.
863 E. Meadow Road
Eden

The Stroh Brewery Co.
4791 Schlitz Avenue
Winston-Salem

Ohio
Anheuser-Busch, Inc.
700 East Schrock Road
Columbus

The Hudepohl Brewing Co.
Fifth & Gest Sts.
Cincinnati

Miller Brewing Co.
2525 Wayne Madison Road
Trenton

The Schoenling Brewing Co.
1625 Central Parkway
Cincinnati

Oregon
Columbia River Brewery
1313 NW Marshall
Portland

G. Heileman Brewing Co., Inc.
1133 W. Burnside Street
Portland

Hillside Brewery & Public House
1505 SW Sunset Boulevard
Portland

Portland Brewing Co.
1339 N.W. Flanders Street
Portland

Widmer Brewing Company
1405 North West Lovejoy
Portland

Pennsylvania
Jones Brewing Co.
Second St. & B & O RR.
Smithton

Latrobe Brewing Co.
P.O. Box 350
Latrobe

The Lion, Inc.
5 and 6 Hart Street
Wilkes-Barre

Pittsburgh Brewing Co.
3340 Liberty Avenue
Pittsburgh

The Stroh Brewing Co.
P.O. Box 2087
Allentown

C. Schmidt & Sons, Inc.
127 Edward Street
Philadelphia

Straub Brewery, Inc.
Rear 303 Sorg Street
St. Marys

D. G. Yuengling & Sons, Inc.
S.E. Cor 5th & Mahantongo Sts.
Pottsville

Tennessee
The Stroh Brewing Company
5151 Raines Rd., E.
Memphis

Texas
Anheuser-Busch, Inc.
775 Gellhorn Drive
Houston

G. Heilman Brewing Co., Inc.
6001 Lone Star Blvd.
San Antonio

Miller Brewing Co.
7001 South Freeway
Fort Worth

Pearl Brewing Co.
312 Pearl Parkway
San Antonio

Pearl Brewing Co.
3301 Church St.
Galveston

Reinheitsgebot Brewing Co.
1107 Summit Ave. #2
Plano

Spoetzl Brewery, Inc.
603 E. Brewery Street
Shiner

The Stroh Brewing Co.
1400 West Cotton St.
Longview

Virginia
Anheuser-Busch, Inc.
2000 Pocahontas Trail
Williamsburg

Chesapeake Bay Brewing Co.
1373 London Bridge Rd.
Virginia Beach

Washington
General Brewing Co.
615 Columbia St.
Vancouver

Hale's Ales, Ltd.
701 N. Main Street
Colville

Hart Brewing, Inc.
P.O. Box 1179
Kalama

G. Heileman Brewing Co., Inc.
3100 Airport Way South
Seattle

Independent Ale Brewing, Inc.
4620 Leary Way, NW
Seattle

Kemper Brewing Co.
P.O. Box 4689
Rollingbay

Kufnfrbrau
112 N. Lewis Street
Monroe

Pabst Brewing Co.
P.O. Box 947
Olympia

Yakima Brewing & Malting Co.
25 N. Front St.
Yakima

Wisconsin
G. Heileman Brewing Co. Inc.
1000-1028 South Third Street
La Crosse

Hibernia Brewing, Ltd.
318 Elm Street
Eau Claire

Jos. Huber Brewing Co.
P.O. Box 277
1208 14th Avenue
Monroe

Jacob Leinenkugel Brewing Co.
1 and 3 Jefferson Avenue
Chippewa Falls

Miller Brewing Co.
3939 W. Highland Blvd.
Milwaukee

Pabst Brewing Co.
917 W. Juneau Avenue
Milwaukee

Sprecher Brewing Co., Inc.
730 W. Oregon Street
Milwaukee

Stevens Point Beverage Co.
2617 Water Street
Stevens Point

"In the neighborhoods of New York, we all grew up on beer. We sat out on the steaming summer nights on rooftops or stoops, drinking beer in cardboard containers. You met your first girls over beer in joints like the Hut or Boops or the Caton Inn; gallons of it flowed from the taps at Rockaway or Oceantide, or under the umbrellas at Scoville's. A couple of Rheingolds, a *News* and a *Mirror*, and the Dodgers beating the Giants and all was right with the world."

—*Pete Hamill,*
"Beer Crisis," New York Post,
February 21st, 1973

"He that buys land buys many stones,
He that buys flesh buys many bones,
He that buys eggs buys many shells,
But he that buys good ale
    buys nothing else."

—*John Ray*
English Proverbs